Teamwork
Test Prep

READING AND MATH

GRADE

5

by Drew Johnson and
Cynthia Johnson

Illustrations by Tim Foley

Carson-Dellosa Publishing Company, Inc.
Greensboro, North Carolina

Credits

Authors: Drew Johnson and Cynthia Johnson
Editors: Kelly Morris Huxmann, Kathryn Wheeler, and Karen Seberg
Layout Design: Mark Conrad
Production: River Road Graphics
Inside Illustrations: Tim Foley
Cover Design: Annette Hollister-Papp

ISBN: 0-88724-258-8

 **Table of Contents**

 # Introduction

Across the country, thousands of students and teachers spend countless hours preparing for state standardized tests. This focus on repetitive, high-intensity preparation can increase student anxiety, cause "burnout," and lead students to develop strong negative feelings about testing—all undesirable effects that can ultimately hurt students' test performance.

Teamwork Test Prep offers a change of pace. This book provides fun, creative group activities that sharpen students' test-taking abilities, build their confidence, instill positive attitudes toward the tests they are facing, and provide them with a supportive network of classmates who share their goals.

Teamwork Test Prep is an effective alternative to the drills and drudgery often associated with the process of getting students ready for standardized tests. It provides everything you need to transform test preparation from a necessary chore into a group experience that is rewarding in its own right. Here is what you will find inside this book:

✗ A short history of the rise of state testing programs

✗ A list of resources where you can find more information about your state's tests and learning standards

✗ An explanation of our unique "teamwork" approach to test preparation and your key role as "coach"

✗ Short, reproducible diagnostic tests to measure your students' current abilities and gauge their progress

✗ Important test-taking skills and strategies that students can really use

✗ Engaging group activities specifically designed to hone important reading and math skills

✗ Practice tests that help students prepare for the real thing

Use *Teamwork Test Prep* as a self-contained test preparation program or supplement your existing program with the activities and diagnostics in this book. Either approach is sure to give your students a boost—in their scores, spirits, and confidence!

 # Understanding Your State's Tests

Understanding the issues involved with state assessment tests is the first step in preparing your students for success. Although standards may vary from state to state, many important issues are common to all states when it comes to standardized testing. The practical information found in this chapter can be used by teachers anywhere in the United States. It includes:

- ✗ The basic components of the No Child Left Behind Act
- ✗ An overview of the test development process at the state level
- ✗ A checklist of questions to help you familiarize yourself with your state's tests
- ✗ Valuable resources you can use to gather more information about your state's tests

The No Child Left Behind Act

Passed in January 2002, the No Child Left Behind Act (NCLB) represents the federal government's most recent plan for education reform. The centerpiece of the law mandates annual testing in reading and math, beginning in 2005, for all public school students in grades three through eight. Although this is a federal mandate, the government has not established a concurrent set of national standards that all states must follow. Instead, states have the flexibility to create their own "statewide accountability systems." Within these systems, each state typically:

- ✗ Sets academic standards in each content area for what students should learn and master at each grade level
- ✗ Develops tests that are aligned with the standards
- ✗ Uses those tests to collect objective data to analyze how students are doing (and often to show how various socioeconomic subsets are faring in the educational system)
- ✗ Makes improvements in curriculum, instruction, and assessment on the basis of test results

Whatever systems the state chooses to develop and follow, it is ultimately held responsible for the performance of its students. Students must perform at a proficient level—according to each state's standards—within 12 years of NCLB's enactment. Each state must also share its data or test results with local communities in the form of reports. These reports are designed to inform parents and other stakeholders of how student learning is measuring up to the state's standards and educational goals. Consequences of the testing results may differ from state to state. In one state, a low-performing district that shows no improvement might have its superintendent replaced, while in another, a school with continued "failing" grades might find itself taken over by the state education agency.

Since many states already have some form of state testing, the passage of No Child Left Behind has not drastically changed current testing patterns. Tests are being revamped, however, to meet NCLB requirements. Since each state has flexibility in setting its own standards, the tests students will take are likely to reflect what they already know or are currently learning. For example, a standardized math test established for fifth graders in Illinois would be relevant for students in that state, but not necessarily for fifth graders in California.

How State Assessment Tests Are Developed

The first step in developing state assessment tests is to establish learning standards. This helps ensure equal learning opportunities for all students and, thus, equal opportunities for academic achievement. Standards are usually divided by grade level and content area or discipline, and some are further divided by course number or subdiscipline. These standards form the basis of the scope and sequence of skills assessed, and in some cases delineate actual content covered, as in social studies or science.

Standards developed in each state set the tone for instruction and achievement. Most state standards reflect carefully derived expectations of what students should know and be able to do at a specific grade level. These expectations of proficiency also establish curriculum frameworks. Educators use these standards as a scaffolding to determine the skills, content, and processes that students should learn.

After the standards are established, the actual test development process begins. Although the process varies from state to state, test development generally goes through several stages. Each state's department of education or state educational agency has a specific internal department or division dedicated to curriculum development and assessment. This group of professional educators first evaluates any previous state assessments to see how well they measure current or newly adopted standards. Then, through analysis of similar or previously administered exams and current assessment research, these educators develop testing blueprints to best represent the core standards and essential elements of the curriculum.

The next stage for most states involves developing field tests based on these blueprints. Field tests are written and administered to try out items that may be used later on actual tests. After the field tests have been administered, review committees evaluate the results to determine the appropriateness, accuracy, and alignment of test items.

Benchmark tests may also be developed to set the scoring goals for new assessments or standards. Like field tests, benchmark tests are scored and recorded, but they are not used for accountability purposes at the district, school, or student level. These tests are used to see how well students will perform on the final tests and to help guide instruction.

The actual writing of the tests can vary depending on the state. Some states develop the tests completely within their own education departments. Assessment specialists review and revise test items, which are written by professional item writers hired independently by the education department. Some states, such as Texas and New York, hire former or current teachers to develop test items using blueprints created by their education departments.

In other states, the tests are outsourced and written by professional educational testing companies that have contracted with the state. Test items are written by company-hired professional writers or, in some cases, by professional writers collaborating with education department staff. These writers use the previously developed test blueprints as guidelines for writing. Each item is written to measure specific content standards and then reviewed by the state's education department for alignment and accuracy.

Once benchmark tests have been developed and administered to students, a passing standard is established on the basis of the results. This passing standard is used to compare how well students should perform versus how well they actually do perform on the real tests.

Finally, the real tests are developed and administered to students. If students do not perform at or above the passing standard, schools use the results to examine factors that may help improve students' scores and, along with them, academic achievement.

Checklist: What You Need to Know about Your State's Tests

Having the information you need about your own state's tests is crucial to your students' achievement. Luckily, this information is readily available. Use the following checklist of questions as a guide in learning about your state's standards and assessment tests:

- [ ] What are the learning standards for each major content area per grade level?
- [ ] What are the most current forms of assessment tests administered at each grade level?
- [ ] What is the state's time frame for developing and administering new assessment tests?
- [ ] What is the schedule of testing dates for each grade level?
- [ ] How are the standards assessed for each test at each grade level?
- [ ] What scoring and rating systems are used for the tests?
- [ ] How and when are testing "report cards" disseminated?
- [ ] Is there any additional pre- and post-testing data available?
- [ ] What test preparation materials are available? (test samples, instructional materials, benchmark or other practice tests, etc.)
- [ ] What training is available at the school, district, state, and regional levels for teachers and parents?
- [ ] What are the implications and consequences of the test results for students, teachers, schools, and districts?
- [ ] Who composes the tests and what input may you have on their design?
- [ ] What local, state, regional, and national resources are available that address standardized testing? (organizations, educational boards and agencies, advocacy and research groups, professional and community listservs, Web-based bulletin boards, etc.)
- [ ] Whom can you contact at the school or district level for more information? (school dean of instruction, instructional specialist, department chairperson, other administrators, etc.)

The Information You Need: Resources for State Standards and Assessment

Much of the information for the checklist on page 7 is available from the following resources:

National Resources
No Child Left Behind Act Web site
http://www.ed.gov/nclb/landing.jhtml
> This Web site includes separate sections for students, parents, teachers, and administrators. It addresses testing, accountability, reading issues, teachers' roles, and much more. The site also provides links to an E-mail based subscription newsletter, details on policy and legislation, fact sheets, statistics and graphs, state testing information, and additional resources.

United States Department of Education
http://www.ed.gov/index.jhtml
> This site contains information for students, parents, teachers, and administrators on educational priorities, research and statistics, PreK–12 issues, as well as links to other educational resources.

National Education Association
http://www.nea.org/
> The NEA's site includes information on accountability and testing, help for parents, a legislative action center link, various publications, and current educational news.

Education News
http://www.educationnews.org/
> This Web site offers free, education-related information from all states, complete with daily headline stories and a searchable archive.

Teachvision.com
http://www.teachervision.fen.com/lesson-plans/lesson-10279.html
> This site provides an extensive list of resources on No Child Left Behind.

State Education Departments/Agencies
An asterisk (*) denotes a special Web site outlining standards/assessments if available.

Alabama Department of Education
50 North Ripley Street
P.O. Box 302101
Montgomery, AL 36104
Phone: (334) 242-9700
http://www.alsde.edu/html/home.asp

Alaska Department of Education and
    Early Development
801 West Tenth Street, Suite 200
Juneau, AK 99801-1878
Phone: (907) 465-2800
Fax: (907) 465-3452
http://www.educ.state.ak.us/home.html
* *http://www.educ.state.ak.us/standards/*
* *http://www.educ.state.ak.us/tls/assessment/*

Arizona Department of Education
1535 West Jefferson Street
Phoenix, AZ 85007
Phone: (602) 542-5393 or (800) 352-4558
http://www.ade.state.az.us/
* *http://www.ade.state.az.us/standards/*

Arkansas Department of Education
#4 Capitol Mall
Little Rock, AR 72201
Phone: (501) 682-4475
http://arkedu.state.ar.us/
* *http://arkedu.state.ar.us/actaap/index.htm*

California Department of Education
1430 N Street
Sacramento, CA 95814
Phone: (916) 319-0800
http://goldmine.cde.ca.gov/
* *http://goldmine.cde.ca.gov/statetests/*

Colorado Department of Education
201 East Colfax Avenue
Denver, CO 80203-1799
Phone: (303) 866-6600
Fax: (303) 830-0793
http://www.cde.state.co.us/index_home.htm
* *http://www.cde.state.co.us/index_stnd.htm*

Connecticut State Department of Education
165 Capitol Avenue
Hartford, CT 06145
Phone: (860) 713-6548
http://www.state.ct.us/sde/

Delaware Department of Education
401 Federal Street
P.O. Box 1402
Dover, DE 19903-1402
Phone: (302) 739-4601
Fax: (302) 739-4654
http://www.doe.state.de.us/index.htm
* *http://www.doe.state.de.us/AAB/*

Florida Department of Education
Office of the Commissioner
Turlington Building, Suite 1514
325 West Gaines Street
Tallahassee, FL 32399
Phone: (850) 245-0505
Fax: (850) 245-9667
http://www.fldoe.org/
* *http://www.firn.edu/doe/curric/prek12/*
  frame2.htm

Georgia Department of Education
2054 Twin Towers East
Atlanta, GA 30334
Phone: (404) 656-2800 or (800) 311-3627
Fax: (404) 651-6867
http://www.doe.k12.ga.us/index.asp
* Georgia Learning Connections Web site:
  http://www.glc.k12.ga.us/
  GLC Phone: (404) 651-5664
  GLC Fax: (404) 657-5183

Hawaii Department of Education
1390 Miller Street
P.O. Box 2360
Honolulu, HI 96804
Phone: (808) 586-3230
Fax: (808) 586-3234
http://doe.k12.hi.us/
* *http://doe.k12.hi.us/standards/index.htm*

Idaho Department of Education
650 West State Street
P.O. Box 83720
Boise, ID 83720-0027
Phone: (208) 332-6800
http://www.sde.state.id.us/Dept/
* *http://www.sde.state.id.us/admin/standards/*

Illinois State Board of Education
100 North First Street
Springfield, IL 62777-0001
Phone: (217) 782-4321 or (866) 262-6663
Fax: (217) 524-4928
TTY: (217) 782-1900
http://www.isbe.state.il.us/
* *http://www.isbe.state.il.us/ils/*

Indiana Department of Education
Room 229, State House
Indianapolis, IN 46204-2798
Phone: (317) 232-6610
Fax: (317) 232-8004
http://doe.state.in.us/welcome.html
* *http://doe.state.in.us/asap/welcome.html*

Iowa Department of Education
Grimes State Office Building
Des Moines, IA 50319-0146
Phone: (515) 281-5294
Fax: (515) 242-5988
http://www.state.ia.us/educate/index.html
* *http://www.state.ia.us/educate/ecese/nclb/doc/*
  ccsb.html

Kansas State Department of Education
120 SE Tenth Avenue
Topeka, KS 66612-1182
Phone: (785) 296-3201
Fax: (785) 296-7933
http://www.ksbe.state.ks.us/Welcome.html
* *http://www.ksbe.state.ks.us/assessment/
  index.html*

Kentucky Department of Education
500 Mero Street
Frankfort, KY 40601
Phone: (502) 564-4770 or (800) 533-5372
TTY: (502) 564-4970
http://www.kde.state.ky.us/

Louisiana Department of Education
P.O. Box 94064
Baton Rouge, LA 70804-9064
Phone: (877) 453-2721
http://www.doe.state.la.us/
* *http://www.doe.state.la.us/doecd/reaching.asp*

Maine Department of Education
23 State House Station
Augusta, ME 04333-0023
Phone: (207) 624-6774
Fax: (207) 624-6771
http://www.state.me.us/education/
* *http://www.state.me.us/education/lres/
  homepage.htm*

Maryland State Department of Education
200 West Baltimore Street
Baltimore, MD 21201
Phone: (410) 767-0100
http://marylandpublicschools.org/
* *http://mdk12.org/*

Massachusetts Department of Education
350 Main Street
Malden, MA 02148-5023
Phone: (781) 338-3000
http://www.doe.mass.edu/
* *http://www.doe.mass.edu/frameworks/current.html*

Michigan Department of Education
608 West Allegan
Lansing, MI 48933
Phone: (517) 373-3324
http://michigan.gov/mde/

Minnesota Department of Education
1500 Highway 36 West
Roseville, MN 55113-4266
Phone: (651) 582-8200
*http://www.education.state.mn.us/html/mde_
home.htm*

Mississippi Department of Education
Central High School
P.O. Box 771
359 North West Street
Jackson, MS 39205
Phone: (601) 359-3513
http://www.mde.k12.ms.us/
* *http://marcopolo.mde.k12.ms.us/
  frameworks.html*

Missouri Department of Elementary and
    Secondary Education
P.O. Box 480
Jefferson City, MO 65102
Phone: (573) 751-4212
Fax: (573) 751-8613
http://www.dese.state.mo.us/
* *http://www.dese.state.mo.us/standards/*

Montana Office of Public Instruction
P.O. Box 202501
Helena, MT 59620-2501
Phone: (406) 444-3095 or (888) 231-9393
http://www.opi.state.mt.us/
* *http://www.opi.state.mt.us/Standards/Index.html*

Nebraska Department of Education
301 Centennial Mall South
Lincoln, NE 68509
Phone: (402) 471-2295
http://www.nde.state.ne.us/
* *http://www.nde.state.ne.us/AcadStand.html*

Nevada Department of Education
700 East Fifth Street
Carson City, NV 89701
Phone: (775) 687-9200
Fax: (775) 687-9101
http://www.nde.state.nv.us/
* *http://www.nde.state.nv.us/sca/standards/
index.html*

New Hampshire Department of Education
101 Pleasant Street
Concord, NH 03301-3860
Phone: (603) 271-3494
Fax: (603) 271-1953
http://www.ed.state.nh.us/
* *http://www.ed.state.nh.us/Curriculum
Frameworks/curricul.htm*

New Jersey Department of Education
P.O. Box 500
Trenton, NJ 08625
Phone: (609) 292-4469
http://www.state.nj.us/education/index.html
* *http://www.state.nj.us/njded/stass/index.html*

New Mexico Public Education Department
300 Don Gaspar
Santa Fe, NM 87501-2786
Phone: (505) 827-5800
http://www.sde.state.nm.us/
* *http://164.64.166.11/cilt/standards/*

New York State Education Department
89 Washington Avenue
Albany, NY 12234
Phone: (518) 474-3852
http://www.nysed.gov/home.html
* *http://www.nysatl.nysed.gov/standards.html*

North Carolina Department of
   Public Instruction
301 North Wilmington Street
Raleigh, NC 27601
Phone: (919) 807-3300
http://www.ncpublicschools.org/
* *http://www.ncpublicschools.org/curriculum/*

North Dakota Department of
   Public Instruction
600 East Boulevard Avenue
Department 201
Floors 9, 10, and 11
Bismarck, ND 58505-0440
Phone: (701) 328-2260
Fax: (701) 328-2461
http://www.dpi.state.nd.us/index.shtm
* *http://www.dpi.state.nd.us/standard/index.shtm*

Ohio Department of Education
25 South Front Street
Columbus, OH 43215-4183
Phone: (877) 644-6338
http://www.ode.state.oh.us/
* *http://www.ode.state.oh.us/academic_
content_standards/*

Oklahoma State Department of Education
2500 North Lincoln Boulevard
Oklahoma City, OK 73105-4599
Phone: (405) 521-3301
Fax: (405) 521-6205
http://www.sde.state.ok.us/home/defaultie.html

Oregon Department of Education
255 Capitol Street NE
Salem, OR 97310-0203
Phone: (503) 378-3569
TDD: (503) 378-2892
Fax: (503) 378-5156
http://www.ode.state.or.us/
* *http://www.ode.state.or.us/asmt/standards/*

Pennsylvania Department of Education
333 Market Street
Harrisburg, PA 17126
Phone: (717) 783-6788
*http://www.pde.state.pa.us/pde_internet/site/
default.asp*
* *http://www.pde.state.pa.us/stateboard_ed/
cwp/view.asp?a = 3&Q = 76716&stateboard_
edNav = |5467|*

Rhode Island Department of Education
255 Westminster Street
Providence, RI 02903
Phone: (401) 222-4600
http://www.ridoe.net/
* *http://www.ridoe.net/standards/frameworks/
default.htm*

South Carolina Department of Education
1429 Senate Street
Columbia, SC 29201
Phone: (803) 734-8815
Fax: (803) 734-3389
http://www.myscschools.com/
* *http://www.myscschools.com/offices/cso/*

South Dakota Department of Education
700 Governors Drive
Pierre, SD 57501
http://www.state.sd.us/deca/Index.htm
* *http://www.state.sd.us/deca/OCTA/
contentstandards/index.htm*

Tennessee Department of Education
Andrew Johnson Tower, 6th Floor
Nashville, TN 37243-0375
Phone: (615) 741-2731
http://www.state.tn.us/education/
* *http://www.state.tn.us/education/ci/
cistandards.htm*

Texas Education Agency
1701 North Congress Avenue
Austin, TX 78701
Phone: (512) 463-9734
http://www.tea.state.tx.us/
* *http://www.tea.state.tx.us/teks/index.html*
* *http://www.tea.state.tx.us/student.assessment/
teachers.html*

Utah State Office of Education
250 East 500 South
P.O. Box 144200
Salt Lake City, UT 84114-4200
Phone: (801) 538-7500
http://www.usoe.k12.ut.us/
* *http://www.uen.org/core/*

Vermont Department of Education
120 State Street
Montpelier, VT 05620-2501
http://www.state.vt.us/educ/
* *http://www.state.vt.us/educ/new/html/pubs/
framework.html*

Virginia Department of Education
P.O. Box 2120
Richmond, VA 23218
Phone: (800) 292-3820
http://www.pen.k12.va.us/
* *http://www.pen.k12.va.us/VDOE/Instruction/
sol.html*

Washington Office of the Superintendent
of Public Instruction (OSPI)
Old Capitol Building
P.O. Box 47200
Olympia, WA 98504-7200
Phone: (360) 725-6000
TTY: (360) 664-3631
http://www.k12.wa.us/
* *http://www.k12.wa.us/curriculuminstruct/*

West Virginia Department of Education
1900 Kanawha Boulevard East
Charleston, WV 25305
Phone: (304) 558-3660
Fax: (304) 558-0198
http://wvde.state.wv.us/
* *http://wvde.state.wv.us/csos/*

Wisconsin Department of Public Instruction
125 South Webster Street
P.O. Box 7841
Madison, WI 53707-7841
Phone: (608) 266-3390 or (800) 441-4563
http://www.dpi.state.wi.us/index.html
* *http://www.dpi.state.wi.us/dpi/dlsis/currinst.html*

Wyoming Department of Education
2300 Capitol Avenue
Hathaway Building, 2nd Floor
Cheyenne, WY 82002-0050
Phone: (307) 777-7675
Fax: (307) 777-6234
http://www.k12.wy.us/index.asp
* *http://www.k12.wy.us/eqa/nca/pubs/
standards.asp*

 **Introducing the Tests to Your Students**

Before tackling any new task, it is a good idea to come up with a game plan for how to proceed. Figuring out a game plan and conveying it to your students can make the task of test taking seem more manageable and even fun!

This book outlines the steps for developing a test-preparation game plan and gives you the tools you will need along the way, including innovative activities and sample test questions. The approach you use in preparing your students, however, will be key to their success. This book's game plan is designed to draw upon your strengths as an encouraging and motivating teacher—in short, as a testing "coach."

Adopting the role of a coach will aid you in helping your students overcome obstacles they face in preparing for state tests. Since these tests are not usually the most enjoyable experiences for students, using the "coach approach" can help eliminate test anxiety, build confidence, develop skills, and increase motivation.

This chapter will explain how to get students started on the right foot by presenting state standardized tests as important challenges students can train for as a team.

The Coach Approach

The activities in this book are designed to build upon and enhance skills that are assessed on state standardized tests in a way that is active, engaging, stimulating, and fun. Remember—test preparation does not have to be boring. Move beyond the usual "skill and drill" and get creative in your approach to teaching. Put on your coach's cap and get your students excited about achieving their test-taking goals.

Coaching can be viewed as the application of teaching strategies to a set of activities that introduce, reinforce, and synthesize skills that players (students) need in order to perform their best. The role involves juggling many tasks at once. As a coach, you are an instructor, a facilitator, a motivator, a troubleshooter, and a supporter, all in one. The role also implies a strong desire to do the job and do it well.

As a good coach, you will motivate your students to do their best, giving them the confidence to work on skills that need improvement. Coaching is a long-term process, requiring both dedication and flexibility. A successful coach will be:

✗ Patient
✗ Positive
✗ Motivated
✗ Resourceful
✗ Creative

Devising a Game Plan

A good coach plans ahead in order to prepare the team for victory. After you have determined your individual approach to coaching, the next step is to develop a game plan. A successful game plan will include activities and exercises targeted to the particular needs of the team. By focusing on areas where students need a boost, you will help them evolve from a scrappy set of inexperienced players to an accomplished team of testing aces. Here is an overview of the instructional game plan outlined in this book:

X Assess students' abilities through diagnostic tests (Chapter 3).

X Set realistic goals for the team using the diagnostic results.

X Use these goals to develop objectives for skill development.

X Strengthen these skills by using specific reading and math activities (Chapters 5 and 7).

X Involve the team in new approaches that use more than one skill at a time (Chapters 5 and 7).

X Simulate the "game environment" through test scrimmages and practice testing scenarios (Chapters 3, 6, and 8).

X Incorporate strategies that strengthen skills and performance (Chapter 4).

X Evaluate the process and teach students how to evaluate how they are doing (Chapter 4).

Before devising a training program, the coach must discern where the players are and where they need to go in order to be successful. That is why we recommend starting your program with the checklist and diagnostic tests in Chapter 3. By first assessing your students' skills and their familiarity with the format of standardized tests, you will be able to formulate an appropriate and realistic plan to help them best prepare for the tests ahead. Using this plan, you can then select suitable activities to work on particular skills and present meaningful strategies for students to apply during the tests.

When introducing your state's tests to students, establish your role as coach from the beginning. Explain that you will be working with the students to figure out where they are in order to get them where they should be before the "big games" that lie ahead. Make it clear that along the way, you will be showing them several strategies they can use in their weaker areas when they feel trapped with the ball, so to speak.

Describe the tests not as something impossible to beat, but as something students can handle on their own. The training program you are developing, based on the students' "pre-event trials" (the diagnostic tests in Chapter 3), will help prepare them well for the tests. Explain that you will also help them stay motivated and maintain a positive attitude toward the tests throughout the program. Make it clear that you welcome any ideas they have to make the process more fun and less tedious.

Cross Training in the Classroom

Since you want to avoid burnout that can happen through basic drill instruction, and since you are an innovative coach by nature, try cross training your academic athletes.

In the usual sense, cross training means varying a regular exercise routine with different forms of exercise to reach the same goal. For example, soccer players may lift weights, football players may take up ballet, and runners may try bicycling to vary their workouts. These different types of activities give athletes new strengths and skills that make them better at their primary sports.

Cross training is an important facet of the coaching philosophy. It can easily be applied to training your students to face testing challenges. Drilling students with practice questions is an important part of test preparation, but it can become monotonous and boring. Cross training can keep students from getting bored. If students are given a variety of methods for developing testing skills, they will learn to apply their skills in different contexts, adapt their strategies to different activities, and synthesize these skills and strategies more naturally when performing on tests. Chapters 4, 5, and 7 of this book address methods of cross training and provide ways to change up the normal "training program" for your students. Here are a few suggestions taken from those chapters:

✗ Intermingle straight drills with activities.

✗ Use different or unusual content to teach skills that cross disciplines. (For example, rather than using a story to teach how to find the main idea, try a popular song, magazine ad, or science article instead.)

✗ Engage students in activities that practice and develop more than one skill at a time.

✗ Set aside some time to teach students methods they can use to deal with test anxiety.

✗ Mix up the skills. Rather than concentrating on reading standards for weeks on end, slip in a math-oriented activity or something that deals with other standards your students are learning in school.

✗ Take a break from training. Avoid overtraining by planning "rest days" when the goal is to have fun learning something new or to try something different.

A beginning team may need to start with simple objectives before moving up to the goal of winning or defeating the opponent. From this standpoint, a good coaching strategy involves building on individual skills incrementally. Having students exercise several skills at once can also help keep tedium on the sidelines while encouraging a more integrated application that reflects the real world. This book provides some activities that focus on just one particular standard or skill, as well as others that tie related skills together in integrated ways.

The Mental Game: Motivation, Metacognition, and Modeling

One of the most important aspects of coaching is motivation. Motivated students have an edge when faced with any academic challenge. Give your students plenty of compelling reasons to want to do well on state tests and boost their self-confidence by preparing them thoroughly. If they see a reason to do well and believe they can learn the necessary skills, students will be well prepared and focused on testing days.

Coaching also involves constant evaluation—of progress, of problems, and of the process itself. Helping students develop metacognitive skills, or making them aware of their own progress and process, will pay off enormously. Use the test-taking strategies in Chapter 4 to teach your students how to think about what they are doing while they are doing it and to identify their own strengths and weaknesses. Encourage them to use their minds to reduce anxiety and alleviate fears about testing. Using metacognition throughout the test-preparation process will help students stay focused and remain in control during the tests.

Another way to help students psych themselves up for testing is to model a positive attitude toward the process. Try not to let any frustrations you may have about the tests dampen your students' motivation. As a coach, you should remain positive and encouraging during training. Encourage team spirit by talking about each test as a big game. Explain that you are going to prepare the students by giving them the techniques, strategies, and experiences needed to give a peak performance. And when introducing the activities in this book, describe exactly how they will help students become better, stronger test-takers.

Standardized tests are a fact a life for students today. Those bound for college will encounter even more high-stakes tests. Your job as a coach is to teach students how to tackle those tests with confidence. You can remove the often crippling obstacles of anxiety and uncertainty from your students' paths, but it will take some work. The activities, strategies, and sample tests in this book, coupled with your own persistence and creativity as a coach, will work together to boost students' skills and confidence.

How Coaching Looks in the Classroom

Since coaching is an active and involved role, any instruction related to your state's standardized tests should be, too. The activities in this book reflect this hands-on approach and provide lots of modeling potential. Each activity has been broken down into the following categories, allowing you to guide students through it step-by-step: Skills/State Standards, Description, Materials You Need, Getting Ready, Introducing the Activity, Modeling the Activity, Activity in Practice, and Extensions.

The activities are designed for collaborative pair or group work. Many are adaptable, however, and can be used with individual students for more focused skill instruction. No matter how you decide to use them, the activities are student-centered in nature, allowing you, the coach, to facilitate and assess while students actively develop their skills.

Identifying Problem Areas

In order to develop a program that will bring your students to peak performance on state assessment tests, begin by identifying any problem areas in their skill development. This will save you time and energy in the long run, and make the whole experience of preparing for the tests more advantageous for students. The short reading and math tests included in this chapter are representative of fifth-grade state assessment tests. They can be used as diagnostic tools to help pinpoint areas in which students need work.

Before administering these diagnostic tests, it may be helpful to determine what exposure your students have previously had to the look, feel, and content of your state's particular tests. Think about what they do in the classroom that addresses test preparation in some way. Since your state's standards serve as the scaffolding for the curriculum, students should already be learning the content and developing the skills that will be assessed on the tests. They may not necessarily realize, however, that what they are learning directly connects to the tests they will take. Use the following checklist of questions to review the key elements of the tests in connection with your students' current testing knowledge.

Checklist: Evaluating Your Students' Testing Savvy

General Questions

- ☐ Do students have experience with multiple-choice tests?
- ☐ How often do students read or write silently in class?
- ☐ How often do students take tests individually?
- ☐ What forms of standardized tests have students taken this year or previously?
- ☐ Do students have frequent practice using answer sheets to record their answers?

Reading Questions

- ☐ How often do students read expository texts? (articles, interviews, biographies, or personal narratives)
- ☐ What story elements can students identify? (plot, setting, character, main idea)
- ☐ Can students analyze character, including traits, motivations, and changes?
- ☐ How often do students use context clues to determine meanings of words?
- ☐ How often do students read texts to determine the author's purpose? (to entertain, to inform, to express, to influence)
- ☐ Do students use graphic organizers to arrange details and ideas about a text?

Writing Questions

- ☐ How often do students use graphic organizers before writing?
- ☐ How often do students write in response to a text they've read?
- ☐ What are the most frequent forms of writing done by students?
- ☐ What forms of writing do students practice that are mirrored on your state's test?
- ☐ How often do students use dictionaries or thesauruses during the writing process?
- ☐ How often do students use their own experiences or examples to support their ideas in their writing?

Math Questions

- ☐ How familiar are students with basic mathematical operations?
- ☐ How often do students measure to determine area, perimeter, and volume?
- ☐ How often do students apply different number theories and operations depending on context?
- ☐ How often do students create, interpret, analyze, and evaluate graphic representations?
- ☐ How often do students use formulas or equations to solve word problems?
- ☐ How often do students round numbers when estimating?
- ☐ Can students use information given in sequence to determine missing information or identify patterns?

For a tailor-made checklist based on your state's standards, see the information provided by your state's education department or agency on the language arts and math standards for grade five. The Web site addresses at the end of Chapter 1 (pages 8–12) provide links to lists of standards available on-line.

Diagnostic Reading Test—Grade 5

Directions: Read the article. Then, answer questions 1 through 8 on your answer sheet.

A Natural Teacher

(1) Nature has always served as a great source of inspiration to humans. Poets have written about nature's beauty. Artists have captured it in paintings and sculptures, and musicians have sung songs and written music that are based on its seasons, sounds, and creatures. But what about scientists? You may wonder what science can learn from nature. Well, the answer is a lot.

(2) As our world becomes more and more dependent on technology, scientists are looking back to nature in order to move forward. Biomimicry, a growing field in science, applies this idea of learning from nature. The word *biomimicry* literally means to mimic or imitate nature. Scientists who use biomimicry see nature as a source for ideas. They then adapt those ideas to meet human needs. Scientists look at how something works in nature and apply that knowledge to solve problems and create needed products.

(3) Many animals in nature serve as the basis for biomimicry research. For example, spiders may hold the answer to inventing something even stronger than a bulletproof vest. A golden orb weaver spider makes six different types of silk. Each type of silk is used for a different purpose, such as wrapping eggs, catching prey, or spinning a web. The strongest material made by any animal is dragline silk, the slippery substance that a spider uses to spin its web or dangle from a corner.

(4) But the farming of spider silk is not easy. Scientists have been looking for ways to recreate spider silk. Through careful study, experts have found that the glands that produce the silk in a spider are similar to the glands that produce milk in goats. After isolating the genes that make spider silk, scientists inserted those genes into fertilized goat eggs. Once the baby goats grow and produce milk, scientists hope the milk will contain the same ingredients as spider silk. So silk may come from milk!

(5) Although biomimicry might sound like a new wave of scientific study, it has been around for a long time. Even the Wright brothers used their observations of birds to help them invent the first successful flying machine. Wilbur Wright applied what he learned from watching buzzards use their wings to float on air currents. While others tried making airplanes with flapping wings, the Wright brothers invented a machine that used the principles of air lift, which they learned from watching birds in flight.

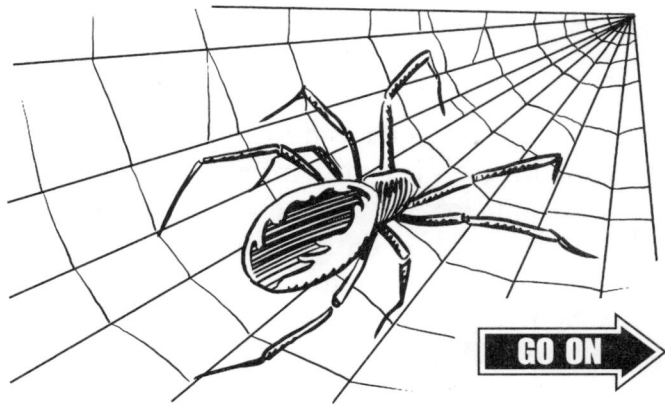

GO ON

(6) Other inventions were also inspired by nature, rather than copying it directly. Did you know that the thorns on bushes inspired barbed wire? Back in 1868, one Texas businessman saw that farmers used thorny plants to contain animals where there was no fencing. Wood for fencing was not widely available, and the bushes took too long to grow large enough to use. So he decided to make a wire with metal thorns to be used for fences. This idea, like many others, worked well. Now over 100,000 tons of barbed wire are sold every year in the United States.

(7) You may be surprised to learn of other familiar products that took their lead from nature. Another common product used on everything from shoes and clothing to bulletin boards and camping equipment is Velcro®. Well, in the early 1940s, one Swiss engineer was tired of picking cockleburs off his pants and from his dog's fur after hiking. Cockleburs are covered with tiny hooks that catch onto the strings in clothing or an animal's strands of hair. After carefully examining how the cockleburs worked to latch themselves onto whatever brushed against them, the engineer developed the Velcro fastener. Thanks go once again to nature for a great idea we still use today.

(8) Even a quiet creature like the sea mussel or gecko could lead to another great product. Mussels use proteins as a super-adhesive glue to stick themselves to rocks in chilly seawater. If scientists can figure out how to make a similar glue, the invention could benefit several industries, from medical surgery to ship repair.

(9) Geckos are also providing insight into developing a hardy reusable adhesive tape. A gecko can leap and climb in all directions without a problem. The reason is the gecko's hairy feet. On its toes are billions of tiny microscopic hairs that work together to stick to a surface through molecular force. A gecko uses these hairs over and over to stick itself to a variety of surfaces. One scientist thinks this idea could be used to develop a reusable adhesive tape strong enough to support an object weighing up to 60 pounds!

(10) We still have a lot to learn from nature, and scientists are finding new ways to use what they learn. Besides making products that are cheaper and better, biomimicry is also helping scientists learn how nature is something to be cared for in order to show the way for future discoveries.

GO ON

1 Read this sentence from the article.

The strongest material made by any animal is dragline silk, the slippery substance that a spider uses to spin its web or dangle from a corner.

What does the word **dangle** mean?

A loop

B weave

C hang

D arrange

2 According to the article, biomimicry is—

F a new wave of scientific study invented by the Wright brothers.

G a method for making goat's milk out of spider's silk.

H a way for scientists to apply ideas from nature to solve problems.

J a business that creates products from nature.

3 What would be a good title for paragraph 3?

A "From a Wave to a Wing"

B "The Secret of Silk"

C "The Mystery of Geckos"

D "Nature Imitates Science"

4 When the author says we still have a lot to learn from nature, he means that—

F nature only has so many ideas to offer scientists.

G scientists can find many answers to problems from nature.

H we must care for nature if we want to benefit from it.

J nature should be used as the basis for all scientific research.

5 A Swiss engineer got the idea for Velcro® from—

A the tiny hairs on a gecko's toes.

B the sticky proteins from a mussel.

C the silk spiders use to spin webs.

D cockleburs on his hiking pants.

6 What was the author's purpose in writing this article?

   F to inform readers about a growing field of scientific research

   G to teach scientists how to make better glue

   H to encourage companies to use animals to make products

   J to make people feel good about the wonders of nature

7 According to the article, which of the following would NOT be an example of biomimicry?

   A studying a gecko's hairy feet to develop a better running shoe

   B watching buzzards float to develop the principles of air lift

   C examining proteins used by mussels to develop a very strong glue

   D observing how farmers used thorny bushes to invent barbed wire

8 Which of the following is a compound word?

   F knowledge

   G adhesive

   H bulletproof

   J ingredients

GO ON

Diagnostic Reading Test—Grade 5 (continued)

Directions: Read the story. Then, answer questions 9 through 16 on your answer sheet.

The Magician and the Pear
A Chinese Folktale

(1) A farmer was making his weekly trip to the village market to sell his pears. His wagon was filled with sweet, ripe pears that everyone wanted to buy. The farmer had many customers that day, causing him to boast, "My pears are the best in the village!"

(2) Soon an old-looking man dressed in torn and ragged clothing came up to the farmer's wagon. The old man looked at the fruit and then asked the farmer for a pear to eat. "All I need is one pear," said the old man, "and I will not bother you anymore."

(3) The farmer tried to get the old man to leave, but he refused. The farmer became so angry he began yelling at the old man to leave, saying, "Why should I give you a pear, when everyone else must pay? Besides, my pears are too valuable to simply give away to any beggar who asks!" The farmer's loud voice caused others in the market to gather around the farmer's wagon and take in the events.

(4) The old man finally said, "Your wagon is full of pears, and all I want is one. Surely you can afford to give me one pear." The crowd watching the scene sided with the old man and tried to convince the farmer to give away one pear for free. However, the farmer's pride had grown as much as his wallet, and he still refused to give the old man a pear.

(5) The market guard who was watching from nearby decided to put an end to the squabble, since the crowd was becoming more restless. The guard dug into his pocket and pulled out a few coins to buy the old man a piece of fruit. The old man thanked the guard, and then said to the crowd, "I am not a greedy man, but a generous one. Let me use my magic to reward all of you with some delicious pears of my own."

(6) The guard then asked, "Now that you have your pear, why don't you just eat it?"

(7) The old man smiled knowingly, and replied, "All I needed was a seed from the pear. I will plant this seed and grow a tree that will produce many juicy pears."

(8) The old man quickly ate the pear, saving a seed in his hand. He took a shovel from the pack he carried and dug a hole. He dropped the seed into the hole and covered it with dirt. Then, the old man asked for some hot water to moisten the ground so the seed could grow. A villager soon returned with a kettle of boiling water, which the old man poured over the ground. Everyone in the market had become fascinated with what was happening. All the people gathered around the old man and the planted seed, forgetting about the farmer and his wagon full of pears.

(9) As everyone's eyes carefully watched the damp ground, a tiny shoot appeared. It quickly grew inch-by-inch and foot-by-foot, until the shoot sprouted branches and became a full-grown tree. The tree suddenly sprouted blossoms over every branch and twig until it was covered with sweet, fragrant flowers. The villagers watched the blossoms become juicy, ripe pears before their very eyes. Without the old man's saying a word, everyone had figured out that he was really a wandering magician.

(10) The magician went up to the tree, picked off the pears, and walked through the crowd, giving away the delicious fruit. Soon the tree's fruit was gone, and the magician had no more to give away. Then the magician took his shovel and began to chop down the tree. After three chops, the tree fell. The magician slung the top of the chopped tree over his shoulder, put his shovel in his pack, and headed out of the village.

(11) During all these events, the farmer had watched in surprise and disbelief, standing in the crowd like anyone else. Once the crowd began to scatter, the farmer returned to his wagon and noticed that it was empty. The farmer became suspicious, thinking that the crowd had stolen his fruit. "But that is impossible," thought the farmer, "because everyone was watching that old man and his tree."

(12) It suddenly dawned on the farmer that the magician had played a trick on him. He realized that the pears the magician had given away were actually the pears from his own wagon! As he stood staring at his empty wagon, the farmer then noticed that the handle of his wagon had been chopped off. The farmer looked everywhere until he found it down the road, lying next to a pile of rocks. He saw that the pear tree the magician had chopped down was really the handle of his wagon. By the time the farmer figured out how he had been tricked, the magician was far down the road, and the villagers were full of the farmer's juicy, delicious pears.

Diagnostic Reading Test—Grade 5 (continued)

9 Read the following passage from the story.

The farmer had many customers that day, causing him to boast, "My pears are the best in the village!"

Which word has almost the same meaning as **boast**?

A offer

B brag

C sell

D speak

10 What happens right after the old man asks the farmer for a pear?

F The farmer gives a pear to the old man so the old man will leave him alone.

G The market guard finds enough coins to buy the old man a pear.

H The crowd makes the farmer feel guilty and he donates a pear to the old man.

J The farmer refuses to give away a pear, and yells at the old man.

11 How does the old man teach the farmer a lesson?

A He uses magic to give away the farmer's pears.

B He takes a pear and turns the seeds into trees.

C He makes the pears become bitter and rotten.

D He chops the handle off the farmer's wagon.

12 Which word BEST describes the magician in the story?

F young

G generous

H greedy

J proud

GO ON

13 What is the main idea of the story?

   A One can never have too much pride.

   B A little generosity can get you into trouble.

   C A little generosity can reap great rewards.

   D Never give away possessions to anyone who asks.

14 Which sentence in "The Magician and the Pear" best shows the farmer's stubborn attitude?

   F The farmer became suspicious, thinking that the crowd had stolen his fruit.

   G "My pears are the best in the village!"

   H "Besides, my pears are too valuable to simply give away to any beggar who asks!"

   J As he stood staring at his empty wagon, the farmer then noticed that the handle of his wagon had been chopped off.

15 What is the meaning of the word **squabble** in paragraph 5?

   A a wandering magician

   B a fragrant blossom

   C a noisy quarrel

   D a clever trick

16 Why did the guard give the old man some coins?

   F He wanted to do a good deed.

   G He had some extra change.

   H He was worried because the crowd was becoming restless.

   J He wanted the old man to perform a magic trick.

END OF PRACTICE TEST

Name: **Date:**

Diagnostic Reading Test—Grade 5

Answer Sheet

Directions: Mark your answers on this answer sheet. Be sure to fill in each bubble completely and erase any stray marks.

1	(A)	(B)	(C)	(D)
2	(F)	(G)	(H)	(J)
3	(A)	(B)	(C)	(D)
4	(F)	(G)	(H)	(J)
5	(A)	(B)	(C)	(D)
6	(F)	(G)	(H)	(J)
7	(A)	(B)	(C)	(D)
8	(F)	(G)	(H)	(J)
9	(A)	(B)	(C)	(D)
10	(F)	(G)	(H)	(J)
11	(A)	(B)	(C)	(D)
12	(F)	(G)	(H)	(J)
13	(A)	(B)	(C)	(D)
14	(F)	(G)	(H)	(J)
15	(A)	(B)	(C)	(D)
16	(F)	(G)	(H)	(J)

Diagnostic Math Test—Grade 5

Directions: Use your answer sheet to record your answers for numbers 1 through 15.

1   Brian and Melissa are making confetti eggs for the school carnival. Melissa has made $3\frac{1}{2}$ dozen eggs, and Brian has made $2\frac{3}{4}$ dozen eggs.
If they need to make a total of 12 dozen eggs, how many eggs do they still need to make?

  A   33

  B   42

  C   69

  D   144

2   Dontae had 6 quarters, as shown below.

He spent 2 quarters on lemonade and 3 quarters on a bag of popcorn. What fraction of the quarters does he have left?

  F $\frac{1}{3}$

  G $\frac{2}{3}$

  H $\frac{1}{6}$

  J $\frac{5}{6}$

3   Wendy is making a wall hanging out of different shapes. First, she drew and cut out a rectangle with a perimeter of 21 centimeters.

> Perimeter = 21 cm   3.5 cm

What is the area of the rectangle?

  F   10.5 cm²

  G   14 cm²

  H   21 cm²

  J   24.5 cm²

4   In the year 1950, California had a population of 10,586,223.

Which statement is true about the number 10,586,223?

  A   The 5 is in the hundred thousands place.

  B   There are 6 ten thousands.

  C   The value of the 8 is 800,000.

  D   The digit in the thousands place is odd.

GO ON ➡

Diagnostic Math Test—Grade 5 (continued)

5   Adele has a book of math puzzles. To figure out the pattern for one puzzle, Adele must multiply and subtract numbers. The table below shows Adele's work.

Steps of Pattern	Multiply	Subtract	Answer
1	2 x 1 = 2	2 – 1 = 1	1
2	2 x 2 = 4	4 – 1 = 3	3
3	2 x 3 = 6	6 – 1 = 5	5
4			

Given the pattern in the table, what is the answer for step 4?

A   2

B   7

C   9

D   8

---

6   What fraction of the circle is shaded?

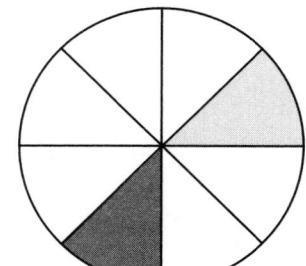

F $\frac{1}{2}$

G $\frac{1}{4}$

H $\frac{3}{4}$

J $\frac{6}{8}$

7   Which expression is NOT the same as 6 x 4?

A   6 x 2 x 2

B   6 + 6 + 6 + 6

C   4 x 4 x 4 x 4 x 4 x 4

D   4 x 6

GO ON ⟹

Diagnostic Math Test—Grade 5 (continued)

8 The graph shows some areas of the school library.

Which library area is best represented by the ordered pair (3, 5)?

F Checkout Desk

G Reference

H Computers

J Fiction

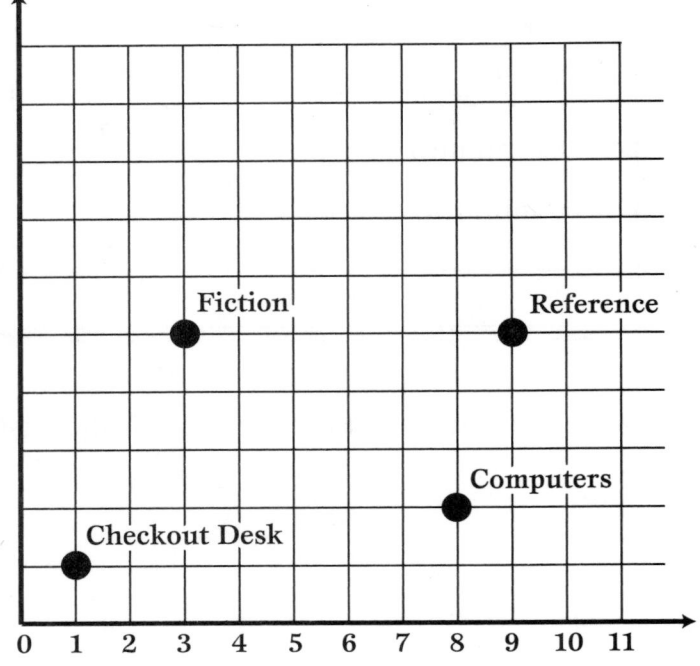

---

9 During one week, Martin walked his dog after school on 4 days. On Monday he walked the dog for 88 minutes, on Tuesday for 42 minutes, on Wednesday for 37 minutes, and on Thursday for 51 minutes. Which is the best estimate of the total number of minutes that Martin walked his dog that week?

A 175 minutes

B 205 minutes

C 220 minutes

D 250 minutes

10 Holly spent $24.50 on art supplies. She purchased 2 canvases for $12.25 each. She then had $7.25 left. Which number sentence can be used to find out how much money Holly started out with?

F ___ = $24.50 – 2($12.25)

G ___ = $24.50 + 2($12.25)

H ___ = $7.25 + 2($12.25)

J ___ = $24.50 – 2($7.25)

GO ON

Diagnostic Math Test—Grade 5 (continued)

11 Sarah is planning to meet Nicole at the movie theater for the 4:30 P.M. show. If the current time is 2:45 P.M., how much time does Sarah have until the show?

A 45 minutes

B 105 minutes

C 90 minutes

D 145 minutes

12 Look at the figure below. Which statement about the figure is true?

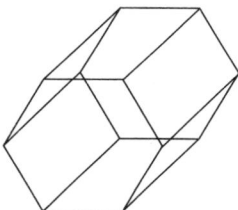

F The figure has two hexagonal faces.

G The figure is a polygon.

H The figure has six faces.

J The figure has no vertices.

13 Kyle wants to buy some skates that cost $150. He has already saved $75. What percent of the $150 does he still need?

A 15%

B 25%

C 75%

D 50%

14 Casey is entering the track meet as a long jumper. In practice, Casey jumped the distances shown in the chart below.

Casey's Jump Distances

Jump	Distance (Meters)
1	2.3
2	2.7
3	2.4
4	2.6

Considering these results, what is the probability that Casey's next jump will be at least 2.5 meters?

F $\frac{1}{4}$

G $\frac{1}{3}$

H $\frac{1}{2}$

J $\frac{3}{4}$

15 Which units would you use to measure the length of a butterfly's body?

A yards

B meters

C centimeters

D feet

STOP

END OF PRACTICE TEST

Diagnostic Math Test—Grade 5
Answer Sheet

Directions: Mark your answers on this answer sheet. Be sure to fill in each bubble completely and erase any stray marks.

1 Ⓐ Ⓑ Ⓒ Ⓓ

2 Ⓕ Ⓖ Ⓗ Ⓙ

3 Ⓐ Ⓑ Ⓒ Ⓓ

4 Ⓕ Ⓖ Ⓗ Ⓙ

5 Ⓐ Ⓑ Ⓒ Ⓓ

6 Ⓕ Ⓖ Ⓗ Ⓙ

7 Ⓐ Ⓑ Ⓒ Ⓓ

8 Ⓕ Ⓖ Ⓗ Ⓙ

9 Ⓐ Ⓑ Ⓒ Ⓓ

10 Ⓕ Ⓖ Ⓗ Ⓙ

11 Ⓐ Ⓑ Ⓒ Ⓓ

12 Ⓕ Ⓖ Ⓗ Ⓙ

13 Ⓐ Ⓑ Ⓒ Ⓓ

14 Ⓕ Ⓖ Ⓗ Ⓙ

15 Ⓐ Ⓑ Ⓒ Ⓓ

 # Test-Taking Skills and Strategies

As your students' testing coach, your role is twofold: to give students the knowledge they need to do well on the tests and to equip them with strategies they can use to refuel, relax, or refocus in order to reach the finish line. This chapter outlines several strategies students can apply to problems that may surface when taking tests.

Getting students into the right frame of mind for testing is one of the most challenging tasks facing a coach. This chapter contains guidelines on how to approach any standardized test and includes test-taking strategies your students can use. Some of your students may be taking standardized tests for the first time. Teaching them these skills and strategies now will give them a great foundation for taking tests throughout their years in school. This chapter is broken down into the following sections:

- ✗ Reducing Test Anxiety
- ✗ General Test-Taking Hints and Strategies
- ✗ Reading Strategies
- ✗ Writing Strategies
- ✗ Math Strategies
- ✗ Before the Test

The boxed "Coaching Clues" that appear throughout this chapter offer suggestions for additional practice or related activities. Some activities have accompanying reproducible handouts. These reproducible pages are arranged by strategy beginning on page 49.

Reducing Test Anxiety

When faced with standardized tests, students may experience a range of reactions, including anxiety. To help students replace test anxiety with confidence, talk about the tests, familiarize students with the test format and structure, and give them techniques to deal with any stress or distractions that may occur during testing.

You may want to begin by asking students to reflect on their own attitudes toward tests. Discuss the different feelings that the prospect of taking a test may trigger, as well as how students might deal with those feelings. Ask students to share any strategies they already use when taking tests.

> *Coaching Clue* — Using the *Testing Questionnaire* reproducible (page 49) as a starting point, encourage students to discuss and reflect on the testing process.

The more familiar students are with the tests they will take, the less stress they will likely experience. One way to help reduce test anxiety is to make students so familiar with the test format that they are comfortable when faced with the actual tests. Pages 34 and 35 include several ways to familiarize students with your state's tests.

Break It Down

Review one or more previously released benchmark or practice tests developed by your state's education department. (See Chapter 1, pages 8–12, for related resources.) Divide the tests into sections and ask groups of students to analyze the format, content, language, and style of each section. Have students look specifically at the directions, types of reading passages and/or test questions, and the total number of questions. Also, point out text features used on the tests, such as titles, illustrations, maps, charts, and graphs. Once all of the groups have shared their findings, review the major points about each test and make a chart to post for reference.

> **Coaching Clue** — Use the *Meet Your Reading Test* and *Meet Your Math Test* reproducibles (pages 50 and 51) to help guide students as they analyze your state's tests. Answer the questions yourself beforehand so that you can add to your students' findings as applicable.

Be a Copycat

Design assignments, quizzes, and tests in the same layout and format as your state's tests. If the reading test includes a variety of text structures, incorporate those same structures into any tests or projects in your curriculum. For example, if students are required to read everything from interviews to letters to the editor, have them rewrite story information in those formats or test them on content using those types of text structures. If your state's math test uses a particular font for numbers or if the graphics are done in a distinctive style, replicate that on any quizzes or assignments that you create based on your curriculum.

Test Experts

Have your students write sample questions in the same format as the tests. These sample questions can be based on texts they are currently reading or on math concepts they are learning in class. Let the students test each other using their sample questions.

Tip Trade

Students may already have some tricks up their sleeves when it comes to dealing with testing issues. Prior to the tests, help students brainstorm different tricks or hints they use to deal with stress, pacing, guessing, and other test-related topics. Then, have them teach these skills to one another in small groups or to the entire class. As a follow-up, give students opportunities to practice these new skills either with practice tests or tests written by the students themselves. (See "Test Experts" above.)

Make It Real

Common sense tells us that the more preparation we have before attempting something, the better we will do. In the same vein, testing experts state that the more exposure students have to practice tests and bubble-style answer sheets, the better they will do on the actual tests.

With this in mind, don't skimp on creating testing situations similar to the "real thing." Although you don't want to reach testing overload with students, you do want them to confidently use what they have learned. Creating authentic test simulations can help both you and your students work out any kinks in the process while strengthening their skills and building their confidence.

Coaching Clue — To help students prepare for testing and to give them experience applying their test-taking skills, create a variety of testing scenarios. Write descriptions of different testing situations or problems to read aloud to the class. While you are reading, have student volunteers act out the actions being described. Then, ask students to offer suggestions of what to do to solve the problems or deal with any obstacles presented in the scenarios.

Before the actual tests, give students a chance to experience an authentic simulation of the testing process. You could use the practice tests included in Chapters 6 and 8 or sample tests from your state's education department. Alternatively, design your own test that has the look and feel of the state tests but that contains content recently learned by the students in class.

Coaching Clue — Some schools hold simulation days where students throughout the school take benchmark or trial tests. Use these simulations as opportunities for discussion with your students about their test-taking experiences. Make sure students realize that a low score on a practice test is nothing to get upset about. Instead, a low score should be seen as an excellent way to spot areas that still need improvement before the actual test.

After students have taken a few practice quizzes and tests, have them analyze the test-taking experience. Use the *Talking It Over* reproducible (page 52) as a guide for this activity.

General Test-Taking Hints and Strategies

While elaborate test-taking strategies may be confusing, there are several straightforward tips and strategies that will help students tackle standardized tests with confidence. This section covers the following key topics:

✗ Pacing Yourself

✗ Making Smart Guesses

✗ Marking Your Answers Correctly

You will know which strategies will be the most useful to your students, so take the time to review the strategies before teaching them. As you present each strategy, answer any questions students have about using the approach in an actual testing situation.

Pacing Yourself

While the majority of state standardized tests are timed, your own state's tests may not be. But regardless of time limits, pacing can play a key role in a student's testing success. Pacing can help students stay on track by helping them focus their concentration, maintain their stamina, and offset any anxiety.

To introduce the concept of pacing, have students envision the tests as a series of track-and-field events. Each part of the test is like a different event. Even if students want to get the best time or highest score for one event, pacing their energy and concentration to handle all of the events will produce a better overall result. Have them practice and employ the following strategies to bolster their endurance and even out their tempo during testing.

X-O Strategy

A steady pace ensures the best performance. Sometimes, however, a student will come across a question that stumps him, causing him to lose his sense of rhythm. Most students approach questions as if they have to be done in order. When they see hard questions, they get stuck and refuse to move on. And the longer they stay stuck, the more anxious and frustrated they become. This is a strategic mistake. Students' scores and attitudes will both get a boost if they make two or three passes through a test, each time skipping questions that seem too hard and going back to them after they have tried to answer all of the other questions.

The X-O strategy is a simple way to maintain a good pace and maximize scores. When working through a section, a student should first take the time to solve or answer any questions she can. If she starts to struggle with a confusing problem and spends more than a few minutes on it without coming up with an answer, she should stop and mark an "X" in the margin next to the question. This is a "maybe" question. The student could probably figure out the solution if she spent more time on it, but for now she needs to move on and try to answer other easier problems.

If the student comes to a question that initially makes no sense to her at all, she should mark an "O" in the margin. This is a "guessing" question. Using strategic guessing techniques can help improve the odds of the student selecting the correct answer on this type of question.

After the student has answered every question she can, she should return to the X questions first and try them again. If they still give her trouble, she should apply strategic guessing techniques, such as the process of elimination (discussed on pages 38–39), to eliminate any incorrect answers. Once some of the possible answers have been eliminated, the student can make an educated guess. After the student has tried to answer all of the X questions, she should go back to the O questions and apply the same strategic guessing techniques.

The X-O strategy keeps students from freezing up when faced with tough questions. It also encourages them to answer every question, and that will ultimately help their scores.

> ***Coaching Clue*** — Practice this strategy with students using the *X-O Strategy* reproducible (page 53) and a previously released benchmark or practice test.

Time-Outs

Most experts believe that the average person can only handle 45 minutes of learning new material before reaching complete absorption. This belief is the reasoning behind the "45/15" rule: after 45 minutes of study, take a 15-minute break. Why not apply this same rule, in a modified form, to taking tests? Tell students that if they need to take time-outs during a test, they should consider taking a break after each section of the test or after a certain length of time.

Most state assessment tests are several hours long. Students understandably find it difficult and uncomfortable to remain in the same position for a very long time. To help students combat desk fatigue, teach them how to do stretches while sitting at their desks. The two exercises described below are written so that you can read them right off the page to your students.

Four-Square Neck Stretches

1. Sitting straight in your chair, tilt your head forward. Try to touch your chin to your chest. Hold for five counts.
2. Tilt your head backward and look up at the ceiling. Let the back of your head rest on the base of your neck while keeping your shoulders relaxed. Hold for five counts.
3. Tilt your head to the right, bringing your ear close to your right shoulder. Hold for five counts.
4. Tilt your head to the left, bringing your ear close to your left shoulder. Hold for five counts.

Shoulder Roll and Pull

1. While seated at your desk, roll both shoulders forward in a circular motion. Continue for a count of ten. Try to keep your neck relaxed. Concentrate on rotating your shoulders in circles rather than just lifting them straight up and down.
2. Switch direction and roll your shoulders backward, also for a count of ten.
3. Next, clasp your hands together and extend your arms out from your chest, as if you are getting ready to hit a volleyball with your forearms. Concentrate on separating your shoulder blades, pulling the muscles in your upper back away from the center and out toward your hands. Hold for five counts.

Making Smart Guesses

Even though state assessment exams do not normally feature a guessing penalty, this does not mean that students should just guess randomly. Encourage students to use strategic guessing strategies instead. Explain how these strategies can help them choose smart answers and, in turn, raise their scores.

Make it clear to your students from the start that guessing is not cheating. Even if they think they have no idea what the correct answer to a question could be, remind them that they have multiple tools on hand to tackle the question. They can use prior knowledge and experience, as well as what they just learned by reading a passage or thinking about a problem. These tools, combined with smart guessing, can help students figure out what the correct answer is.

Although the X-O strategy (see page 36) can help students pace themselves throughout a test, it can also be used as the first step toward guessing strategically. If students begin by first answering the questions they definitely know, they can then go back and deal with the remaining questions using smart guessing and the process of elimination.

POE: Process of Elimination

Applying POE, or the process of elimination, during a test simply means weeding out any unsuitable answer choices. The inherent beauty of multiple-choice tests is that the correct answers are always provided—students just have to learn how to identify them.

Students are often amazed and encouraged when you explain that the right answers are in plain view in their test booklets. To get students comfortable with POE, first explain that the answers are all there on the page. Then, show them how the process works. Write a sample question and list answer choices such as the following on the board or on an overhead transparency:

Carolina is drawing with a felt-tip marker. How long is her marker?

A	2 inches
B	6 inches
C	12 inches
D	36 inches

Even without measuring the marker, students can come up with a likely answer to this question. Ask them to think about how big most markers are. Then, have them consider each of the answer choices:

- Choice A is too short. How many markers have they seen that are only two inches long? Students can eliminate or cross out choice A.

- Choice D is equal to three feet. Three feet is too long to be the length of a marker! Have students eliminate that choice as well.

- Choices B and C both seem somewhat likely. They are in the range of what a normal marker's length would be. But, option C is equal to one foot. That seems a bit too long. If students were to guess at a correct answer, they would probably choose answer B, which in this case is correct.

Point out to students that although they did not actually know the answer to this question, they were able to use their brains to cross out options and make a good guess. Remind students that if they can eliminate the obviously wrong answers, they will have a much better chance of guessing the right one.

Coaching Clue — This kind of reasoning can be applied to many standardized test questions with excellent results. Try this as an exercise with students by tailoring the steps outlined previously to address a sample problem from one of your state's practice tests.

Critical Words and POE

As they apply the steps of POE, advise students to look for any critical (or extreme) words in the questions or answer choices. These words, which are often underlined, italicized, boldfaced, or set in all caps, may help students narrow down their choices or guide them in the right direction. Have them circle or underline any extreme words, such as the following:

NEVER	ONLY	ANY
EXCEPT	BEST	ALL
ALWAYS	NOT	NONE

Explain how these words can help them eliminate answer choices when common sense and prior experience are not helping. Very often, though not always, answer choices with extreme words in them are wrong. If a student is forced to guess, you can advise her to cross out choices that include critical or extreme words.

Flip a Coin

If a student has narrowed down the answer options as much as possible by eliminating wrong or unlikely choices but still has two or three possible answers, he should just pick an answer—guess and move on. The odds are that over the course of the test, he will guess correctly at least some of the time, thus improving his score. Completely random guessing should be discouraged, however, because it gives students the feeling that they can just give up and guess on hard questions when, in fact, a little POE and deductive reasoning could help them get close to the right answers. The fact is, unless there is a guessing penalty on your state's tests, students have nothing to lose by guessing. Tell them to answer every question but to guess blindly only if they have exhausted all of their smart guessing strategies.

Marking Your Answers Correctly

Nearly all standardized tests require students to record their answers by filling in some form of lettered bubbles. As with anything else, the more experience students have in using bubble answer sheets, the more natural the process will be during the actual tests. Give students the practice they need by incorporating bubble-style answer grids into everyday activities, from daily warm-ups to homework review or pop quizzes.

One of the pitfalls of skipping a question in the test booklet is that a student may forget to skip that problem on the answer sheet. Having students use simple bookmarks or rulers while testing can help them stay on top of which problems they are skipping and need to go back to later. Check your state's guidelines to see if additional tools such as these are allowed during the tests.

Another approach is to have students record their choices on the answer sheet after they have finished each section. This reduces the risk of filling in the bubbles incorrectly. Just tell students to write or circle their final answer choice for each question in the test booklet itself. Then, after each section, they can transfer their answers to the answer sheet.

Coaching Clue — To help students become comfortable recording answers on bubble or grid sheets, provide opportunities for students to practice using them. Include directions and bubble sheets similar to those on your state's tests for students to use with short quizzes or other classroom assignments. Be sure to answer any questions that students have about the process.

Reading Strategies

Purposeful Reading

Before reading something, we usually internalize our reasons for reading it. For example, we determine whether we are reading to get information, to be entertained, to learn something, or to explore another side of an issue. When students look at a text, they may not consciously think about why they are going to read it. They may think only that it is something they have to read. For greater comprehension and better results, encourage students to have a purpose in mind when reading, especially when they will be required to answer questions about a text.

Questions, Questions, Questions

If students are familiar with the different types of questions they may encounter on a test, they will likely be better able to answer them. Review and explain the most familiar types of questions well in advance of the real tests. Reading questions can generally be organized into three categories: Instant Recall, Pause and Look, and Reader and Passage.

Instant Recall Questions — These are basic "right there" questions that ask students to recall information stated in the text, usually in specific places. Examples: "What color was Jennifer's balloon?" or "Who invented the lightbulb?"

Pause and Look Questions — These questions ask students to pause after reading, think about what they read as a whole, and look for information in the passage that connects to the question. The answer may not be found in one particular place in the text, but rather in an overall combination of details. Example: "What is one difference between the king and the servant?"

Reader and Passage Questions — These questions require students to apply what they already know in connection to what they have just read in the passage. These are the most challenging questions because they involve higher-level thinking, such as making inferences, drawing conclusions, making comparisons, or interpreting character. Example: "How did Jake feel when his dog was stolen?"

Coaching Clue — Using practice tests as a guide, ask students to brainstorm the types of questions that could be asked on your state's standardized reading test. Organize the questions by type in a chart for student reference.

Once students are familiar with the different types of questions, prompt them to offer potential questions about a specific text. What kinds of questions might a test writer ask about what they just read?

The Mystery of Text Structures Revealed

Students can also use text structure to help them find answers to questions. If students understand how a text is structured, they can focus on looking in a particular part of the text to answer a question efficiently and accurately. For example, the basic structure of a story has a beginning, a middle, and an end. Usually in the beginning portion of a story, the setting, characters, and other basic details are introduced to the reader. If a question following the passage asks for the name of a character or where the story takes place, students should know to look for clues in the beginning part of the story. On the other hand, if there is a question about a problem, the details will probably be found in the middle of the story.

Coaching Clue — Read and discuss various text structures in class. Then, have students work in teams to write questions related to specific sections of a passage. Have the teams exchange questions, then explain where in the passage each answer would most likely be found.

Graphic Organizers

More and more reading tests ask students to complete graphic organizers using information from texts. The types of organizers on the tests are similar to those that students use to organize their thoughts before writing. Some of the most common types of organizers students may be asked to complete include:

✗ Venn diagrams or compare/contrast charts
✗ Clustering organizers like webs or brainstorming charts
✗ Sequence maps or chain-of-events flowcharts
✗ Story maps

One of the best ways to prepare students for dealing with graphic organizers is to use them frequently and fluidly in class. Demonstrate how to use the organizers with a variety of text structures. For example, a cluster or webbing diagram could be used to list details from a nonfiction passage on dolphins, as well as to show the attributes or choices of a character from a folktale. When asking students to compare two characters, have them complete a Venn diagram or a compare/contrast chart.

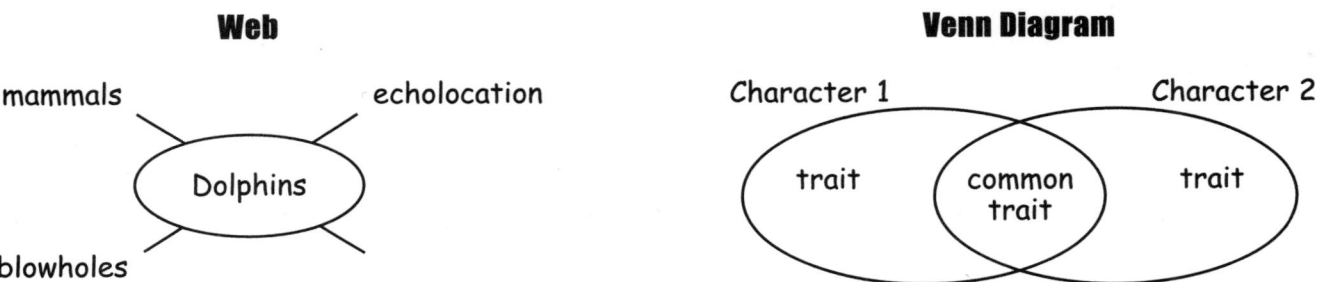

SQ3R Revamped

Most teachers know SQ3R as an effective technique for retaining and comprehending reading material, but it can also be applied to test taking. Students can use an adaptation of this method when dealing with reading selections on standardized tests. This modified strategy can be used with chapter books, textbooks, and expository texts, as well as short stories and other narrative passages.

Teach students to apply this modified version of SQ3R when approaching a reading selection and related questions on a test:

SKIM
QUESTION
READ
RESPOND
REVIEW

4

SKIM the passage before reading

✗ Look at the title. What does it tell you about the selection?

✗ Look at any illustrations, photos, captions, graphs, or maps.

✗ Read through and label the questions before reading the passage.

Note: Some may argue that skimming can cause students to miss the subtleties of what the questions are really asking because students may just look for the answers rather than read the whole passage. Familiarizing themselves with the questions first, however, can help students focus on what the reading passage may be about. If students read the passage from beginning to end with the questions already in mind, it is similar to having a teacher provide them with a study guide of ideas, questions, or concepts to guide the reading they do in class.

QUESTION while skimming

✗ Turn the title into a question to help get you interested in the subject. For example, if the title is "An Ancient Disk's Secret Message," change it into a question to focus your reading: "What is the ancient disk's secret message?"

✗ Think about what you already know about words in the title or the subject of the passage. Try to connect your own knowledge and experience with the text you will be reading.

Note: Part of examining the title is to get students thinking about what they already know about the subject of the selection. If students are not sure what the passage is about, they can look at the words they do understand in the title and in the title question. What does the word "ancient" mean? What about "secret messages"? When might secret messages have been used? Could this be an old form of messaging? Maybe it's an earlier version of a computer disk—an ancient disk?

READ the passage actively

✗ Read with a purpose. Based on the title and other clues gleaned from skimming the passage, why are you going to read it? Why did the author write it in the first place? The major purposes are to inform, entertain, persuade, and express.

✗ Read carefully and at a comfortable pace, thinking about the questions, new information you discover, and what you already know about the subject.

✗ Mark up the text. As you read, underline phrases that stand out, make you think about something, or relate to one of the questions. Circle words you don't know or think might be important. Write your comments, questions, or ideas about the reading in the margins of the text.

43

RESPOND and REVIEW

✗ Read through the questions, answering the easiest ones first. If you are unsure about any questions, apply the X-O strategy.

✗ Circle or underline any critical words in the questions and answer choices. Paraphrase each question by saying to yourself, "I'm actually looking for . . ."

✗ Use the process of elimination to eliminate any answer choices you know are wrong. Cross out any choices that you know are not right, and then reread the choices that are left. Try to narrow it down to no more than two choices for each question.

✗ Make an educated guess between the two answer choices that remain. If necessary, reread the passage for any clues or ideas about the answer.

Coaching Clue — Use the *Modified SQ3R* reproducible (page 54) as a reference when discussing this strategy with your students.

Writing Strategies

While some states have writing tests for all grades, others have tests for alternating grades (grades 6 and 8 or grades 5 and 7, for example). Check with your state's education department or agency to determine if a writing test will be administered at the fifth-grade level.

Graphic Organizers

Graphic organizers are great ways to help students organize their thoughts during the prewriting process. Encourage students to practice using the organizers in class. The more practice they have, the better prepared they will be for the tests. Some graphic organizers useful for the types of writing prompts that students may encounter on the standardized tests include:

✗ KWL charts
✗ Venn diagrams or compare/contrast charts
✗ Clustering organizers like webs or brainstorming charts
✗ Sequence maps or chain-of-events flowcharts
✗ Story maps

K What I Already **K**now	W What I **W**ant to Learn	L What I **L**earned
Platypuses are mammals that lay eggs.	What does the word platypus mean?	Platypus comes from Greek and means "flat-footed."

ROW Strategy

Since writing is thinking on paper, preparing students for the writing portions of standardized tests means preparing them to express their thoughts in written form. To help your students think before they write, have them follow the ROW strategy: Read/Rephrase, Organize, and Write.

READ/REPHRASE

Read the prompt, circling or underlining any key words, such as *describe*, *compare*, *explain*, or *support*. Rephrase the prompt to make it clearer or easier to understand. Think of the purpose for writing and what structure to use.

ORGANIZE

Use a graphic organizer to collect your thoughts before writing. Pull specific details or quotations from the text and think of examples from your own experiences to back up your points. Record this information on the organizer.

WRITE

Using the graphic organizer as a guide, write your essay.

Knowing How to Respond

One key strategy in writing an effective response to a prompt is determining what type of response to write. This seems pretty straightforward, but understanding the terms used and what they mean is crucial for students when planning their responses.

> **Coaching Clue** — Use the *Chart of Writing Terms* (page 55) to review with students the key descriptors they may see on writing tests for their grade level.

Math Strategies

Turning Words into Numbers

Word problems can present a major challenge for students. Not only do students have to understand and know how to use the math, they also have to figure out how the words translate into mathematical equations before they can begin to solve the problems.

To help students make the transition from learning math concepts and skills in isolation to seeing math in real-world contexts, try to incorporate words and writing about math throughout the curriculum. Asking students to describe a problem-solving process using words rather than numbers, keep a learning log of processes, and translate number sentences into word-based relationships will give them lots of practice in this area.

Coaching Clue — Use the newspaper or other expository texts as resources for potential word problems. As students read for information, have them come up with their own word problems. Another option is to have them create word problems based on numerical problems from a textbook. For more ideas or an activity on this type of skill-building strategy, see the math activities in Chapter 7.

Using different problem-solving strategies with students will also help them better transform words into numbers in order to reach solutions. Some of the most common problem-solving strategies used at the fifth-grade level include:

- ✗ Drawing a picture to describe the problem
- ✗ Acting it out
- ✗ Making a table, chart, or graph
- ✗ Working backward from the solution
- ✗ Looking for a pattern
- ✗ Guessing and checking (using number sense and POE)
- ✗ Working a simpler problem

Coaching Clue — For practice, give students several word problems and have them apply a variety of problem-solving strategies to each problem in order to find a solution. Discuss how certain word problems lend themselves more easily to different solution strategies, and ask students to keep this in mind when solving word problems on the tests.

Words That Reveal Mathematical Operations

Certain words indicate certain mathematical operations. With your students, take a close look at sample word problems taken from class assignments or practice tests. Have students pick out the key words or phrases in each problem and discuss what operation each indicates.

Coaching Clue — Distribute copies of the *Math Vocabulary Chart* reproducible (page 56) for students to use as a reference. Make an additional copy of the chart on a transparency. Ask students to use their charts to record any new words they find in word problems that indicate particular operations. Have the students share their findings, and record the results on your transparency.

Using Number Sense

Emphasize common sense, or number sense, with your students as part of the problem-solving process. When they look at a problem and the answer choices, students can use number sense to help visualize the correct amount, dimensions, or shapes asked for in the problem. Encourage students to use number sense to eliminate erroneous choices before even beginning to work the problem. For example, look at the following word problem:

> Monica is shopping for holiday presents. She has $40 to spend.
> She bought one pair of shoes for $25. How much money does she have left?

> A $40
> B $25
> C $15
> D $5

Students can use visualization and basic number sense to eliminate two answer choices right away—A and D. They can then apply basic problem-solving steps to do the math and choose the right answer. This process is similar to POE, described earlier in this chapter. The difference is that number sense is like common sense and should be used whenever dealing with problems involving realistic mathematical situations.

RIDDOTS Strategy

After they have become fluent word-problem translators, teach students to use the RIDDOTS strategy when completing a real test on their own. This strategy is pretty straightforward and can be modeled with a variety of word problems that students may see on your state's tests. RIDDOTS is an acronym that stands for the following process: Read, Identify, Determine, Omit, Translate, and Solve.

Read the entire problem carefully.

IDentify any key words that will help you solve the problem.

Determine what you need to find out.

Omit unnecessary details.

Translate the words into an equation.

Solve the problem and choose an answer.

Coaching Clue — Use the *RIDDOTS Strategy* reproducible (page 57) to guide students through an example and help them better understand how to use this strategy.

Before the Test

The weeks before testing are perfect for reminding students that they are ready to handle whatever comes their way. It is also a great time for getting them excited about doing well on the tests. Here are just a few suggestions for boosting your students' confidence and enthusiasm as the tests draw near:

- ✗ Hold a pep rally in your classroom. Have students write cheers, give pep talks, and make signs and banners to hang in the classroom for motivation.

- ✗ Have a T-shirt design contest, where students create logos or graphics and slogans. Hold a fund-raiser to raise money to buy and print the winning design on the shirts. Students can wear the shirts during the tests.

- ✗ Do something completely different the day before the test. By now, your students should be ready. Give them a needed break by doing something less taxing and more recreational—maybe a hands-on activity or game that involves movement and creativity rather than drill-and-practice.

Top Five Test-Taking Tips for Students

Finally, give students these five tips to remember before, during, and after the tests.

1. **Be confident!**
   Remember that you are prepared to do well. You have been "working out" to get ready for the tests and can succeed. It's time to show what you can do.

2. **Be prepared!**
   Get a good night's sleep, eat a hearty breakfast, and wear clothes suitable for testing—comfortable layers you can take off or put on in case the testing room is too hot or cold. Bring all of the materials you will need, such as pencils, a dictionary, or a calculator.

3. **Review the test before you begin.**
   Before you start, spend a few minutes reviewing the test carefully. Familiarize yourself with each section and then decide how to pace yourself.

4. **Be focused and relaxed.**
   To keep up your concentration, use the test-taking strategies you have learned. If you start to feel tense, take a few deep breaths and do some stretches.

5. **Look over the test when you are finished.**
   Make sure you haven't skipped any sections and that you have answered every question. Check your answer sheet to make sure the bubbles are filled in neatly and correctly. Proofread any writing for proper spelling, grammar, and punctuation.

Testing Questionnaire

Directions: Read each statement. Mark your answer by checking the appropriate box.

ALWAYS	SOME OF THE TIME	NEVER		
☐	☐	☐	1.	When I take a test, I feel confident that I am prepared and will do well.
☐	☐	☐	2.	The night before a test, I get a good night's sleep.
☐	☐	☐	3.	The morning before a test, I eat a good breakfast.
☐	☐	☐	4.	My mind wanders when I'm taking a test.
☐	☐	☐	5.	During a test, I forget what I have learned and then remember it once the test is over.
☐	☐	☐	6.	I make careless mistakes when taking a test.
☐	☐	☐	7.	I check my work and my answers before I turn in a test.
☐	☐	☐	8.	I rush to finish when I take a test.
☐	☐	☐	9.	When taking a test, I think too much about the questions, change my answers a lot, or don't answer at all.
☐	☐	☐	10.	If I don't know an answer, I narrow down my choices and guess.
☐	☐	☐	11.	If I don't know an answer, I skip the question and come back to it later.
☐	☐	☐	12.	During a test, my breathing gets weird or my body feels tense.
☐	☐	☐	13.	If I don't understand a question or what I'm supposed to do on a test, I ask for help.
☐	☐	☐	14.	If I start to lose concentration or get tired, I take a little break.

Directions: Discuss your answers to questions 1–14 with the rest of the class. Then, read each statement below. Mark your answer by checking the box for TRUE or FALSE.

☐ TRUE ☐ FALSE	15.	It is better to guess on a question than to leave it blank.
☐ TRUE ☐ FALSE	16.	Being first to finish a test is better than being last.
☐ TRUE ☐ FALSE	17.	If you get bored or can't concentrate, you should just put your head down and go to sleep.
☐ TRUE ☐ FALSE	18.	It's a waste of time to check your work before turning in a test.
☐ TRUE ☐ FALSE	19.	You should never take a break from a test.
☐ TRUE ☐ FALSE	20.	It's important to relax and stay focused when taking a test.

Meet Your Reading Test

Directions: Together with your team, look at your state's reading test. Answer the questions below, writing your answers on the lines provided. Use a separate sheet of paper if needed.

1. What are some directions that are repeated for each reading selection? _____

   _____

2. Is there room to write, make notes, or underline words in the test booklet? _____

3. How many reading selections are there? _____

4. Are there any pictures or drawings with the reading selections? How might the illustrations help you during the test?

   _____

5. Are any words in the reading selections **boldfaced**, underlined, or *italicized*? _____

6. What are the reading selections about? What types of selections are there? _____

   _____

7. About how many questions follow each reading selection? _____

8. What types of questions are there ("Instant Recall," "Pause and Look," "Reader and Passage")? List about how many of each kind.

   _____

   _____

9. What question formats are used (multiple choice, short response, essay, etc.)?

   _____

10. Are there any critical words in the questions or answers, such as BEST, NOT, or EXCEPT? List a few examples.

    _____

Meet Your Math Test

Directions: Together with your team, look at your state's math test. Answer the questions below, writing your answers on the lines provided. Use a separate sheet of paper if needed.

1. What are some directions that are repeated in each section? _____

    _____

2. Is there a math reference sheet or chart included in the test booklet? _____

3. What kinds of tools are you allowed to use during the test (calculator, ruler, etc.)?

    _____

4. How do you mark your answers for the problems (answer bubbles, bubble grid, etc.)?

    _____

5. Is there space in the test booklet to work through problems? _____

6. How many problems are there in all? _____

7. What types of problems are there? _____

    _____

    _____

8. What types of pictures or graphs are included? _____

9. Which problems seem the hardest? _____

    _____

    _____

10. Which problems seem the easiest? _____

    _____

    _____

Talking It Over

Directions: After taking a practice test, think about how you felt. Then, answer the questions in the boxes below.

Reflecting on the Tests	
What did you find the **most challenging** about the **reading** test?	What **strategies** did you use during the **reading** test?
What did you find the **most challenging** about the **writing** test?	What **strategies** did you use during the **writing** test?
What problems were the **most challenging** on the **math** test?	What **strategies** did you use during the **math** test?

Preparing for the Real Thing	
List the **major skills you want to work on** as you prepare for the **reading** and/or **writing** tests.	List the **major skills you want to work on** as you prepare for the **math** test.

X-O Strategy

Directions: Use the X-O strategy to guide you through the test-taking process. Be sure to mark your test booklet as instructed below and to complete all portions of this handout.

Round 1: Read through the questions or problems on the test. As you read, answer the questions you can complete without too much effort or time. Mark those answers on your answer sheet.

   A. Mark an X by each question or problem that you think you can answer but are not sure about. Record the number of questions marked with an X here: _____

   B. Mark an O by each question or problem for which you would have to guess the answers. Record the number of questions marked with an O here: _____

Round 2: Go back through the test and try to answer all of the questions marked with an X.

   A. If you need to, reread, rework, or review the questions. Look for additional information to help you clarify anything or support the answers you think are correct.

   B. Mark the answers on your answer sheet.

Round 3: Go back through the test and try to answer all of the questions marked with an O.

   A. Note any critical words in the questions. Circle or underline these words and write them on the following lines.

   _____

   _____

   B. Apply POE, or the process of elimination.

   • Use common sense and logical reasoning to eliminate bad or unlikely answer choices. Think about how any critical words can help you determine the answers by eliminating some of the answer choices.

   • Cross out any answer choices that you know are incorrect or unlikely.

   • Try to narrow down the answer choices to two per question.

   C. Use your own prior knowledge, information from the text and any other clues given (such as graphics or illustrations) to make educated guesses. Mark your answers on your answer sheet.

Modified SQ3R

SKIM – QUESTION – READ – RESPOND – REVIEW	
SKIM before reading	• Look at the title, headings, and subheadings. • Look at any pictures, charts, graphs, or maps. • Skim the questions to see what they are asking.
QUESTION while skimming	• Turn the title, headings, and subheadings into questions. • Think about what you already know about the subject. • Write down questions you have in the margins of the text or on a sheet of scratch paper.
READ the **passage actively**	• Read with a purpose. Think about the author's purpose for writing: to inform, entertain, express, or persuade. • Read the captions under any illustrations or graphics. • Mark any underlined, *italicized*, or **boldfaced** words and phrases. • Make notes and underline words, phrases, or sentences that relate to the questions. • Stop and reread any unclear or confusing paragraphs. • Try to get a sense of the main idea of each paragraph and of the passage as a whole.
RESPOND **and REVIEW**	• Answer questions based on what you read. • Reread where necessary. • Use strategies to help you answer the questions.

Chart of Writing Terms

The following chart lists terms frequently used in fifth-grade writing prompts.

Writing Term	Definition — What It Means
Compare	Take a close look at two or more things, characters, events, or ideas. Explain what is ALIKE about them.
Contrast	Take a close look at two or more things, characters, events, or ideas. Explain what is DIFFERENT about them.
Describe	Show rather than tell by painting a picture with words. Create a clear impression of a person, place, object, or event. Include details that relate to all five senses.
Explain	Give the who, what, when, where, why, and how about something. Provide details to make it easily understood.
Narrate (Write a Story)	Use all of the major parts of a story. Include a setting, characters, a beginning (introduction), a middle (problems/events), and an end (resolution/conclusion). Include details and literary elements that make the story interesting and relate them to the prompt.
Persuade	State your view or opinion on a topic. Support your view with examples or reasons from the text or from your own experiences.
Reflect	Look back at or reflect on events, ideas, or your own related experiences. To reflect on something you have read means to think deeply about its meaning.

Math Vocabulary Chart

This chart shows what different words can mean in story problems. In the extra space in each box, add other key math words that you find.

Meaning	Words and Phrases Found in Story Problems		
Add	increased by added to altogether	more than sum	total of combined
Subtract	decreased by fewer than	minus less than	less difference between/of
Multiply	times product of	multiplied by	increased by a factor of
Divide	per ratio of	out of quotient of	percent (divide by 100)
Equals	is/are will be yields	was/were gives sold for	is equal to is the same as

RIDDOTS Strategy

Write a word problem in this space:

Now follow the steps in the left column to complete the boxes in the right column.

Read the entire problem carefully.	
IDentify any key words in the problem and write them in the box on the right.	
Determine what you need to find out: What are you trying to solve? What are you looking for?	
Omit unnecessary details from the word problem.	*Draw lines through words in the problem above that are NOT related to what you need to know or find out.*
Translate the words of the problem into an equation, formula, or mathematical expression.	
Solve the problem. • Show your work. (Use the back of this sheet if needed.) • Choose an answer, if provided. • Write your answer in the box on the right.	

# Skill-Building Reading Activities

This chapter includes 12 different activities designed to help you build and reinforce students' reading comprehension skills. Each activity provides an engaging way for students to practice one or more key skills that will be assessed on your state's standardized tests. Students will be asked to use their knowledge, experiences, and imaginations. Each activity is structured in the following format:

- ✗ Skills/State Standards—breakdown of the skills addressed in the activity
- ✗ Description—brief summary of the activity
- ✗ Materials You Need—list of materials required for the activity
- ✗ Getting Ready—tips for the teacher and a description of what to do in order to prepare for the activity
- ✗ Introducing the Activity—suggestions for introducing the activity and capturing students' interest
- ✗ Modeling the Activity—ideas for demonstrating the activity (if applicable)
- ✗ Activity in Practice—step-by-step instructions for working through the activity
- ✗ Extensions—variations, extensions, and other teaching suggestions

All of the activities are designed to be hands-on and group-oriented, requiring active participation by your students. Also flexible in nature, they can be modified to meet your students' needs and give students individual practice. You can use the activities in any order. You may find that some are more suited to the particular needs of your students than others.

Some activities also include reproducible pages. These pages are found at the end of this chapter, beginning on page 84.

The matrix on page 59 organizes the activities by the predominant skills or standards they address. Some activities address more than one skill and may, therefore, appear under more than one category on the chart.

Matrix of Skills Addressed in Reading Activities

Skill/State Standard	Activity	Page
Comprehension	What's in the Bag?....................60 What Comes Next?....................70	
Story structure and elements	What's in the Bag?....................60	
Determining main idea	Compact Disc Artists.................62	
Summarizing and paraphrasing	What's in the Bag?....................60 Campfire Songs...........................64	
Sequencing and chronology	Time Travelers.........................66 What Comes Next?....................70	
Making inferences and drawing conclusions	Hit or Miss...............................68	
Making predictions	What Comes Next?....................70	
Comparison and contrast	Hot Off the Press!......................72 What Am I?...............................82	
Identifying cause and effect	Time Travelers.........................66 What Comes Next?....................70	
Using context clues	Fictionary.................................74	
Author's purpose	Target: Audience!.....................76	
Analyzing character	Skin Deep.................................78	
Using graphic organizers	Time Travelers.........................66 Get Graphic!.............................80	
Understanding genres	What Am I?...............................82	

What's in the Bag?

Description

The "What's in the Bag?" activity is a new take on the book report format. In this activity, students create a bag of items that represent different elements of a story—characters, setting, major events, and details. The items they collect can be found objects, words, or even their own creations. As students share their bags in a way similar to show-and-tell, they must actively retell the story using their objects as concrete and figurative visuals. Through this sharing, students practice summarizing and demonstrate comprehension.

Skills/State Standards

X Comprehension

X Story structure and elements

X Summarizing and paraphrasing

Materials You Need

- *What's in the Bag?* reproducible (page 84)
- Brown paper lunch bags
- Art supplies (colored markers and pencils)
- Overhead projector and supplies

Getting Ready

This activity can be used for teams or for individual students. Since students may need time outside of class to collect objects for their bags, the activity can be extended over the period of a few days. Assemble a few examples of bags and objects for previously read books and stories. These examples will help students brainstorm on their own. You may also choose to share several example bags from one book, showing a range of objects and their relation to the story. Make student handouts using the *"What's in the Bag"* reproducible and an additional copy on a transparency to use during the modeling portion of the activity.

Introducing the Activity

Show students one of your sample lunch bags. Ask them to guess what is inside the bag—a sandwich? Some chips? An apple or a cupcake? After getting several suggestions, open the bag and pull out objects representing major elements of a story very familiar to students—either one they just read or a common-knowledge one like a fairytale or a book turned into a movie. When the bag is emptied of the objects, ask students what connections they see between the objects. Lead students to see how these objects represent elements of that specific story by holding up each one in turn and having students explain the connection.

Tell students that they will get a chance to fill their own bags with objects to help them tell a story they have read, and then they will share the bags with their classmates. Explain that the objects they choose can be whatever will help them tell the story in the way they want.

Modeling the Activity

1. Using another of your sample bags, model how to tell a story using the objects in a bag. As you tell the story, explain why you chose the objects.

2. If students need further modeling, consider creating a bag of objects related to a story unfamiliar to students. As you tell the story using the objects, encourage them to ask questions for clarification, elaboration, or interpretation.

3. Place the transparency of the *What's in the Bag?* handout on the overhead projector. Using another familiar story or book, ask students to help you complete the transparency for each column. As they offer suggestions for story elements and objects, ask for elaboration and connections between the objects and the elements they represent.

4. Once the chart is completed, ask students to think about how some objects would be easier or better to use than others. For example, in *The Adventures of Huckleberry Finn*, a key object would be a raft. What could they use instead to represent the raft?

5. Clarify that there is no one right way to tell a story for this activity. Emphasize that the important thing is to be thoughtful when selecting objects and to have fun.

Activity in Practice

1. Distribute paper lunch bags and copies of the *What's in the Bag?* handout to students. Have students work individually or in small teams to complete the handout.

2. After they have completed their handouts, have students begin to select the objects they might use to create their bags by circling the best options for each category on the chart.

3. Ask students to decorate the outsides of their bags, either in class or at home.

4. Explain that for homework, students will need to collect the objects for their bags and practice their presentations.

5. When students have completed their bags, have them share their stories with the whole class or in small teams. If sharing in teams, have each team select the best storyteller to share with the entire class. Encourage students to ask questions as they share their stories.

6. After the presentations, ask students how sharing their stories in this activity helped them understand the story more than if they simply wrote a book report about it. Explain that what they did without realizing it was to practice their comprehension skills while internalizing the different elements of a story.

Extensions

This activity can be used to strengthen oral presentation skills. By designing a simple rubric, students can begin by concentrating on basics like projection and clarity, then work up to other speech-related skills.

You may also adapt this activity to work with expository readings. In that context, students will have to identify the major concepts in the text and determine objects that best represent them while summarizing and sequencing.

Compact Disc Artists

Description

Determining the main idea and relevant supporting details is a major skill tested at many grade levels. Providing experiences for students to practice analyzing the relationships between the details and the overarching message is critical for strengthening this skill.

Skills/State Standards

X Determining main idea

In this activity, students use a story's details and main idea to create a compact disc play list. The CD's title represents the main idea with the song titles representing the supporting details.

Materials You Need

- *Compact Disc Artists* reproducible (page 85)
- Examples of music CDs
- Sample CD title and play list for modeling activity
- Overhead projector and supplies
- Stories for practice segment of activity

Getting Ready

Having examples of CDs on hand will help students during the practice segment of the activity.

Make an overhead transparency and student handouts using the *Compact Disc Artists* reproducible.

Introducing the Activity

Ask students to name popular recording artists they know. After getting some suggestions, ask students if they have ever listened to a CD of their favorite recording artist. What were the titles of the albums or CDs? What about the names of some of the songs?

Explain that when recording artists create an album, they think about how all of the songs work together to get their message across. The album's title is like the main idea of the album, and all of the songs help support the title, as do the details in a story or text.

Tell students that in this activity, they will assume the role of a recording artist and create a compact disc based on a story or other text they have read. First, they will identify the text's supporting details. Then, using these details they will determine the main idea of the text and from that generate a title for their CD. Finally, they will shape the supporting details into song titles that relate to the title of the CD.

Modeling the Activity

1. Read the CD titles and accompanying play lists of a few compact discs aloud to students. Discuss as a group how the titles and songs work together to convey the main idea to the listener. Consider listening to some of the songs if time permits.

2. Place the transparency of the *Compact Disc Artists* reproducible on the overhead and complete it, using a story or other text familiar to students. Explain how you looked at the supporting details to come up with song titles and how they helped you think about and determine a CD title representing the main idea.

3. If more modeling is needed, have students help you complete another transparency using the details and main idea from another story they have read.

Activity in Practice

1. Decide beforehand if each team will read a different story or if the whole class will use the same text. This can also be done after reading a story or other text as a class.

2. Divide students into teams and distribute copies of the *Compact Disc Artists* handout.

3. Explain that although they are working in teams, each member should work to complete the handout individually. Later, they will share their ideas to develop a CD title and play list of songs.

4. After each team member has completed the handout, have teams share their ideas and develop a CD title and play list.

5. Once all teams have finished, and if time permits, have them design CD covers.

6. Ask students how this activity helped them determine the main idea and supporting details of a text.

Extensions

To provide additional practice with summarization and theme, students could actually write the lyrics to some of the songs on their CD play list, using details of the story as the basis for the songs' content.

This activity could also be modified to incorporate different conceptual themes—such as a main idea pizza, butterfly, or some other multifaceted object related to a specific story that students have read.

Campfire Songs

Description

Telling a story through song is an age-old tradition. A song format often makes it easier to remember an event, tale, legend, or story by summarizing the main facts and details in a few key verses and refrains.

Teaching students how to summarize through song is a fun and engaging way to give them practice in this skill while accessing prior knowledge, drawing on their creative and musical talents, and exercising their speaking and oral presentation abilities.

In this activity, students work collaboratively to summarize a text and then transform their summary into a song, including verses and refrains/choruses. Their songs can be modeled after the patterns of a familiar tune, such as "I've Been Working on the Railroad."

Materials You Need

- *Campfire Songs* reproducible (page 86)
- Copies of lyrics from traditional songs
- Transparencies of a story summary and a traditional song's lyrics for modeling activity
- Cassette player/recorder and tapes (optional)
- Overhead projector and supplies

Getting Ready

Consider having a packet of traditional song lyrics (those in the public domain) available to use as models when students compose the song summaries in the practice segment of the activity. Make student handouts using the *Campfire Songs* reproducible. Create transparencies of a story summary and lyrics for a traditional song.

Introducing the Activity

Ask students if they know the words to "I've Been Working on the Railroad." After they offer a few lines, ask them to tell you what the song is about—some of the singer's experiences while working on the railroad.

Explain that this and other songs often tell a story in a condensed way, like a musical summary. Offer other examples of traditional campfire songs and ballads to illustrate this.

Tell students that this activity will give them practice in summarizing a story or text by writing a campfire song based on the musical patterns of songs they already know.

Modeling the Activity

1. Review some other familiar campfire songs and ballads with students. Select one and use an overhead transparency to show students how the words on the page come alive when the musical rhythm is added.

2. Next, ask students to help you summarize a story familiar to them. Compare the students' oral summary to your summary written on the transparency.

3. Use a transparency to show how to borrow the pattern of the song selected in Step 1 to create a campfire song about the story summarized in Step 2. On one side of the transparency, list the words to the song. On the other side of the transparency, write your campfire song version, pointing out how each line in the new song mimics the rhythm of the original song.

4. If the song has a chorus or refrain, show students how that can be used to convey the main idea of the story to the listener, since a chorus or refrain is repeated several times throughout the song.

Activity in Practice

1. Distribute copies of the *Campfire Songs* handout. Then have students form small songwriting teams and select a song pattern as the model for their campfire song. To encourage variety, either assign different stories or texts to each team or assign specific song patterns to each team.

2. Have students complete the handout individually and then share their drafts with team members. Have them collaborate on a team version, sharing lines and ideas from each team member's handout.

3. Once each team has created its final song, have students rehearse the songs, deciding which parts will be sung individually and which will be in unison.

4. After rehearsals, collect copies of all the songs to make into a campfire songbook. Then have each team perform its song for the entire class; ask students to sing along using their songbooks.

5. If time permits, consider recording the songs on cassette tape and sharing them with the school library to add to its collection of audio recordings.

Extensions

If using a longer text, each team could be assigned a segment and use a different song for each segment, reflecting the mood and tone of that segment as well as the content.

For advanced practice in summarizing, give students the option of writing a haiku about a text.

Time Travelers

Description

In this activity, students construct meaning by taking discrete events from a text and placing them in the order in which they occur. Working in pairs, students become "time travelers" and go into the text, enacting one event or action for the rest of the class. As the class analyzes the event, students collaborate on where the event should be placed on a large time line, thinking about its causes and effects. After all of the pairs have traveled in the text, the class evaluates the time line for any time lapses or errors in the flow of the text's events. Looking at the relationships between problems and solutions, students will deepen their understanding of the overall text.

> ### Skills/State Standards
> ✗ Sequencing and chronology
> ✗ Identifying cause and effect
> ✗ Using graphic organizers

Materials You Need

- Copies of a text (story, article, etc.) for practice segment of activity
- Large sheet(s) of butcher, kraft, or colored paper for time line
- Index cards
- Overhead projector and supplies

Getting Ready

Students should already have read the text or story that will be used for this activity. If used with a longer text, consider doing the activity after each major section or chapter. Create time-traveler cards, describing a major event from the story on each card.

Introducing the Activity

Ask students where they would go if they had access to a time machine. Would they travel way back in time or would they jump 10 years into the future? Remind them that they travel in time every day, from when they get up in the morning to when they go to bed at night.

Next, ask students to think of three things they did, saw, heard, or felt today. Then ask them to think about the order in which those things happened. Explain that ordering those events in a time sequence is an example of chronology. Give a definition of the word *chronology* and explain how arranging events in the order in which they occur is an important skill to have—one students will practice in this activity.

Tell students that they are about to become time travelers, working with partners to travel into a story they have read. Each traveler pair will act out a part of the text for the class. Then, the class will try to determine where that event occurs in the text. After all of the pairs have acted out their events, everyone will work together to complete a large time line of the events.

Modeling the Activity

1. Select a simple fairy tale and create a small number of time traveler cards that describe a major event on each card. Here is a sample of what might be written on a card:

> ### The Three Little Pigs
>
> Event: Big Bad Wolf blows down the pig's house made of straw

2. Announce the title of the fairy tale. Tell students you are going to travel in time to act out a series of events. Ask for volunteer time travelers to accompany you into the story to help you with each card.

3. After you have enacted one event, use an overhead transparency to label where that event falls on a time line. Make sure the students offer the location.

4. As the remaining cards are enacted, stop after each one to place the event on the time line with students' input. Correct the placement of events as needed.

5. After all of the cards have been enacted, ask students to look at the time line to see if they can pinpoint causes/effects and problems/solutions in the fairy tale.

Activity in Practice

1. Have students help you construct a large paper time line. Tape it to the wall or board.

2. Divide the class into teams of two time travelers. Give each pair of students an event card. Instruct students to be as creative as they want to be as they create their enactments but the event must still be clear to the class.

3. After each pair travels into the text, ask the class where the card should go on the time line. Tape each card onto the time line between time travel sessions. Students may resequence event cards as needed.

4. After all of the pairs have finished, ask students to identify the major causes/effects and problems/solutions in the story while considering their sequence on the time line.

Extension

An advanced version of this activity would omit certain events within a text. After students have enacted all of their time cards, the entire class must work together to determine what events are missing.

Hit or Miss

Description

In this activity, students will practice making inferences while thinking and speaking on their feet. Divided into two teams, students will compete to make inferences from excerpts of a text. In the beginning rounds, possible inferences are given after each excerpt is read. As the game progresses, answer choices may be eliminated altogether, forcing players to make inferences on their own. The team that makes the most correct inferences wins the game. Through this activity, students will come to realize that the secret to unlocking the meaning of a text often lies in a combination of clues from the text and reflection on their own experiences.

Skills/State Standards
- ✗ Making inferences
- ✗ Drawing conclusions

Materials You Need

- Sample inference excerpts from texts (stories, articles, poems, etc.)
- Multiple choice answers for excerpts
- Transparencies of excerpts and answer choices
- Index cards (a different color for each team)
- Overhead projector and supplies

Getting Ready

The excerpts themselves do not need to be very long—probably no more than a paragraph. Finding a good text that includes inferences may take some time. Several excerpts from different stories could also be used. Sequencing the excerpts will depend on how many come from one text and how much of a story the excerpts tell in some way. To make it more challenging, you may mix them up rather than use them in the order in which they occur in the text.

Introducing the Activity

Read students the following sentence: "Jeremy entered the school building just as the tardy bell rang, looking like a wet kitten." Ask them to tell you what happened to Jeremy. After they make a few guesses, ask them why they drew those conclusions.

Break down the process they followed to reach the conclusion they did:
- They listened for clues in the sentence—*tardy bell rang, wet kitten*
- They thought about their own experiences (made inferences) in connection to the clues—
  tardy bell = late for school; that's not good
  wet kitten = cats don't like to get wet; Jeremy probably didn't mean to get wet, either
- They drew a conclusion using the clues and their inferences—Jeremy got caught in an unexpected downpour on his way to school

Tell students that they make inferences every day in order to draw conclusions about things they encounter. For example, if they see someone laughing, they can guess that something must be funny, even if the person laughing doesn't say so. When they read something new, they can also make inferences to help them better understand what is going on in the text. Tell students that they will get more practice making inferences by playing the "Hit or Miss" game in teams.

Modeling the Activity

1. Using the overhead projector, show students a sample excerpt and set of answer choices. See example at right.

2. Next, ask them to vote on the answer they think is most likely. Tell them that although any of the three might have happened, the most likely, considering clues in the text and common experiences, is choice B.

> Excerpt: "Jeremy entered the school building just as the tardy bell rang, looking like a wet kitten."
>
> Which of these most likely happened to Jeremy? Did he—**A.** forget to set his alarm clock?
> **B.** get caught in the rain?
> **C.** try to wash his kitten?

3. Repeat with a few more excerpts until you feel students grasp the process.

4. Remind students that the excerpts in the game will come from real texts, so the skills they use to play the game will be the same skills they will use when reading on their own.

Activity in Practice

1. Divide the class into two teams and let each team choose a name.

2. Explain the rules of the game: For each round, a team will send a player "up to bat." An excerpt and answer choices will be shown on the overhead projector while read aloud by the game show host. Each player makes an inference and draws a conclusion by looking at the excerpt, getting ideas from teammates, and then selecting an answer choice and writing it on an index card. After the answers are written and collected by the host, they are read aloud. Each team has a chance to receive points for each correct answer. Each correct answer is a "hit," and each incorrect answer is a "miss."

3. As the rounds continue, the excerpts can become more challenging, and the answer choices could be eliminated entirely. At that point, players can receive additional points for explaining their answers with evidence from the excerpt (to support both their inferences and following conclusions).

Extensions

The format of this game can be altered to suit your students' needs and ideas, such as a baseball game, spelling bee, or even inference charades.

If students need more individual practice to warm up before this activity, read a series of passages aloud and have students write down their inferences on index cards. Then collect the cards, read the inferences aloud after each passage, and use them to discuss how to use inferences to draw conclusions.

What Comes Next?

Description

In this activity, students work on making predictions about a text while using its major details and events and connecting them in a cause-and-effect pattern. While piecing together a text's meaning, they also exercise their listening and speaking skills.

You will create a series of cards based on the content of a text—it may be the plot of a story, a series of events in a newspaper article, or a series of facts and details from a magazine article or informational passage. The first card contains only a question. The next cards each contain an answer (written at the top or on one side) and a question (written at the bottom or on the flip side). Distribute the cards randomly to students. The student with the first card reads the question aloud as the rest of the class listens and tries to figure out if they have the right answer on their cards. If they think that they do, they can read their answers aloud. The student with the correct answer card can then read the card's question to continue the chain of answers and questions until the final answer is read.

Materials You Need

- Story, book, article, or other text for activity
- Index cards
- Overhead projector and supplies

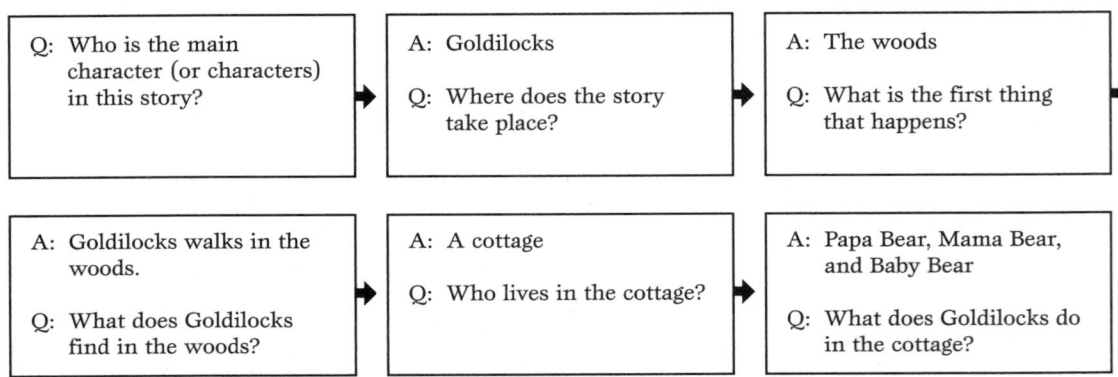

Getting Ready

The trick to getting this game to work well is to write fairly straightforward questions and answers that could fit with one another in many variations, but that make the most sense (and are most accurate) when paired together logically—but not literally—on the cards.

Here is an example of a card chain for the fairy tale "Goldilocks and the Three Bears":

Q: Who is the main character (or characters) in this story?	A: Goldilocks Q: Where does the story take place?	A: The woods Q: What is the first thing that happens?
A: Goldilocks walks in the woods. Q: What does Goldilocks find in the woods?	A: A cottage Q: Who lives in the cottage?	A: Papa Bear, Mama Bear, and Baby Bear Q: What does Goldilocks do in the cottage?

Create a series of cards according to the content of a selected text, using the previous example about Goldilocks as a reference. The number of cards will be determined by the size of your class. This activity also works well with expository texts because of the factual and/or sequential information that can be extended over the series of cards, building upon one another as students read the answers and questions. Before introducing the activity, replicate the answers and questions shown below on a transparency.

Introducing the Activity

Ask students to guess the answer to this question: "Walter Hunt invented what small, practical tool?" After they offer a few answers, ask them to try again. This time use the overhead projector to show students the following sample of answers without revealing the questions.

A-1: sewing machine	A-2: safety pin	A-3: thimble
Q-1: When was the sewing machine patented?	Q-2: For how much did Hunt sell the patent?	Q-3: From what materials were the earliest thimbles made?

After they try again, reveal the three questions, one under each choice. Ask them again what the answer to the first question might be. Lead them to see that the answer should be A-2, since Hunt is mentioned in the next question under that answer. Explain to students that they made a prediction about the answer using the questions as clues. Tell students that they will be making predictions about a text before they read it in this activity. Each of them will have a card containing an answer and a question. Students will listen carefully to the initial question and then decide if they have the right answer on their own cards. If they think that they do, they should say their answers and read their questions. Explain that while they are listening, they will be piecing together the subject of the text they will read. Tell students to think carefully about the causes and effects of what is happening in the text and use them to help decide what comes next.

Activity in Practice

1. Distribute one card to each student. If the text is lengthy or detailed, students may receive more than one card. Either read the first card aloud or to give it to a student to read.
2. After the first card is read, guide students as they read their cards aloud, pausing to redirect them if the cards are not read in sequence. When students have made it through all the cards, do a quick recall by reviewing the questions and answers together.
3. Ask students to make some overall predictions about the text they will be reading. Highlight any causes and effects that were noted on the cards.

Extensions

To exercise their comparison/contrast skills, have students write short predictions of the text after the activity, then compare them with the actual text. This activity can also be used after students have read a text to check their comprehension of story details.

Hot Off the Press!

Description

Comparing and contrasting is a skill students will frequently see on standardized tests, whether they are asked to examine two versions of the same story or to identify similarities and differences between two elements within a particular text.

In this activity, students will compare and contrast two different forms of a text while transforming one into another. Students will take a story and reshape it into a newspaper article. During this process, they must think about the essential elements to include in their translations, consider the differences in purpose between these two forms, and recognize similarities and differences between the two texts.

Materials You Need

- *Hot Off the Press!* reproducible (page 87)
- Copies of newspaper articles
- Copies of stories for activity
- Overhead projector and supplies
- Art supplies (markers, pens, poster boards)

Getting Ready

Provide students with copies of newspaper articles; the stories may give them ideas for their own articles. Decide whether all teams read the same story or separate ones. Make an overhead transparency and student handouts using the *Hot Off the Press!* reproducible.

Introducing the Activity

Ask students to recall the plot of the fairy tale "The Three Little Pigs." Ask them who normally tells the story—one of the characters or a narrator outside of the story's action? Then, lead them to think about what that story would be like if it were told in a newspaper instead. What would be the headline? What type of information would be included? How would the style of retelling the events differ from or be the same as the original version?

Explain that comparing and contrasting details of two versions of a story is an important skill to develop in preparation for the tests they will take.

Tell students that during this activity, they will create their own newspaper articles from a story. They will need to figure out the different details to include, the approach and purpose of the article, and other elements to replicate the style of a newspaper article.

During this process, students will work on comparing and contrasting skills as they think about the differences between the two story versions. Then they will determine what impact these differences have on the reader's understanding.

Modeling the Activity

1. Show students some short newspaper articles as examples for format, headline, content, and purpose. Talk about how any of the "stories" in the articles might translate into actual narrative stories.

2. Use a familiar story as the basis for modeling the process. Place the transparency of the *Hot Off the Press!* reproducible on the overhead projector and complete it with input from students using details from the sample story.

3. After completing the sheet together, show students a sample newspaper article based on the story. Ask students to tell you what the similarities and differences are between the versions and how the reader might gain a different understanding by comparing one version to the other.

Activity in Practice

1. Divide the class into teams. Distribute copies of stories and the *Hot Off the Press!* handout.

2. After each team has read the story, have students work individually to complete their handouts.

3. Next, have students collaborate as they share ideas from their handouts to draft a newspaper article. Post these reminders for students to keep in mind as they work:

Writing a Good Newspaper Article
- Include all essential details
- Start with a good "lead" (first sentence)
- Remember the style of a newspaper article—objective, fact-based, and including quotations from those involved in what happened
- Come up with a headline and any "photographs" for your article

4. Next, have each team of students create a final version of their article using poster board, colored markers, or pencils.

5. After all the news articles are finished, direct the teams to present their work to the class. If all of the teams have read the same story, ask students to note any similarities and differences between the two versions. If each team has read a different story, have each team work together to complete a Venn diagram or compare/contrast chart after presenting their news article.

Extension

This activity could also be done in reverse—give students newspaper articles, and ask them to generate stories in narrative form, using the details and events described.

Fictionary

Description

The simple strategy of using context clues to determine the meaning of an unknown word is one that students need to practice often. In addition, using a dictionary to determine the meaning of multiple-meaning words in relation to their context is of growing importance in terms of how tests are addressing the reading and writing process.

Skills/State Standards

✗ Using context clues

In this activity, students develop their context clue skills while becoming more adept at using a dictionary to expand their vocabularies. In *Fictionary*, a word that is unfamiliar to all of the students is read from the dictionary. Students then listen to a sentence containing the word used in context. Working either in small teams or individually, students create a definition for the unknown word, written in the form of a dictionary definition. After reading aloud all of the possible definitions, students vote on the one they think is the actual meaning. Each team or student gets a point for voting for a correct definition and a point for receiving any vote for their original definition.

Materials You Need

- Dictionary or classroom set of dictionaries
- Sentences with context clues for activity
- Overhead projector and supplies

Getting Ready

If vocabulary is taught through word lists, consider incorporating those words in this activity. Words in reading passages of standardized tests are often above grade level, so keep this in mind when selecting words to use.

Introducing the Activity

Read an unfamiliar word aloud to students and ask them to try to guess its meaning. Then read a sentence aloud that contains that word without any context clues—a very flat sentence. Ask students if they can determine the word's meaning from the sentence. When they respond in the negative, ask them why. Lead them to see that there were no clues in the sentence to help them out. Next, read a different sentence with the same word but that contains helpful context clues. Ask students to point out the difference between the two sentences. Remind students that often when they encounter a word they don't know, they can try to figure out its meaning by looking at the verbal stepping stones—the context clues—around the word.

Tell students that they will act as Word Masters in this game. They will write their own definitions for words they do not know by using the stepping stones (context clues) in sentences to help them navigate their crossing from unfamiliar words to known and "owned" words in their vocabularies.

Modeling the Activity

1. Use an overhead transparency containing sample dictionary entries or a classroom set of dictionaries to review the format of definitions. Consider having students look through the dictionaries and select words and definitions to read aloud as a warm-up activity.

2. Next, model the process by reading aloud an unknown word and writing it on a transparency. Then, write a sentence containing the word and context clues. Finally, write your own definition.

3. Look up and read the real definition aloud to students and write it on the transparency. Then have the students make comparisons between your definition and the dictionary's version.

4. Ask them to tell you what context clues were helpful in determining the word's meaning and writing an original definition.

Activity in Practice

1. Decide whether students will work in teams or individually.

2. Follow the process from the modeling segment by first reading a word aloud and then reading a sentence that contains the word used in context. Consider writing the word and its sentence on a transparency so students may see the clues as well as hear them.

3. Have students write their definitions on separate sheets of paper for each word.

4. After definitions for a word are created, collect them for that word's round, read them aloud, and ask students to vote on which one they think is correct.

5. After revealing the dictionary's definition for each word, ask students to point out the context clues in each sentence.

6. Award points for choosing a correct definition as well as for any votes students receive for their own definitions.

7. At the end of the game, rank the top three students or teams as Word Masters for this game session.

Extensions

If practicing this activity in teams, consider moving toward individual practice by having students generate definitions on their own. A flip version of this activity could also help students with their writing skills—write an unknown word and its definition on a transparency and have students create sentences using the word in context.

Target: Audience!

Description

In this activity, students will make print advertisements for a specific text according to its purpose—to inform, entertain, express, or persuade. During this process, they will determine the text's purpose from its structure

> ### Skills/State Standards
> X Determining author's purpose

and organization and its overall idea. Students will then combine these elements on a one-page print ad (in the style of a promotion for an event or that of a movie poster). For example, if students read a poem and determine that its subject is springtime and it was written to entertain the reader, their advertisement would include elements that reveal the content of the poem as well as its lively and entertaining nature.

Materials You Need

- *Advertising Techniques* reproducible (page 88)
- *Target: Audience!* reproducible (page 89)
- Text selections for modeling and practice segments of activity (one for each team)
- Sample advertisement for modeling activity
- Overhead projector and supplies

Getting Ready

Use one of the text selections as a basis for a sample advertisement. Create a transparency or make copies of the ad for students.

Have lots of samples of print advertisements on hand to help inspire students during the practice segment of the activity.

Use the *Advertising Techniques* reproducible to make an overhead transparency. Make student handouts using the *Target: Audience!* reproducible.

Introducing the Activity

Ask students several questions about the purpose of different types of texts: Why would somebody write a story? Why do people read a newspaper or watch the evening news? Why do we use articles in textbooks and not just stories in school? After students offer ideas and opinions about these types of writing, explain that different types of writing have different purposes—reasons that someone decided to write in the first place. Tell students that in this activity, they will determine the purpose of several types of writing.

Modeling the Activity

1. Explain the major purpose for each type of writing: to inform, persuade, entertain, and express. Offer examples such as newspaper articles, editorials, poems, stories, and letters to the editor.

2. Read with students very short examples of writing that illustrate each purpose. Work together to identify the purpose of each example.

3. Discuss different ad strategies using your *Advertising Techniques* transparency.

4. Review with students the major elements of an advertisement: logo, slogan, product placement, and any other details.

5. Ask students which type of ad would probably work the best for each purpose for a text.

6. Share your sample advertisement with students and go over each part. Ask them questions and review the content, approach, and creative touches that you employed to create your sample ad.

Activity in Practice

1. Divide the students into small ad teams. Distribute copies of the *Target: Audience!* handout and reading selections to students. Make sure each team has a different selection to read.

2. After teams have read their selections, have them work together to complete the handout.

3. Students may use the information from the handout to brainstorm ideas for their advertisement. Offer examples to provide inspiration and ideas for each team.

4. Have teams create rough drafts and then final versions of their advertisements.

5. When all of the teams are finished with their advertisements, make a copy of each for the other teams and distribute them. Have each team look at every advertisement to figure out the purpose of the text forming the basis for the advertisement.

6. After students have offered their views on whether each advertisement successfully characterized the purpose of the text, consider having students vote on the top three advertisements.

7. Have the top three teams discuss how they came up with their ideas for the advertisements based on their reading selections.

Extensions

If time allows, consider adding other types of advertisements to the activity, such as creating a TV commercial or movie poster for the particular selection.

To incorporate comparison and contrast skills, have students explain the similarities and differences in the different types of writing samples and their purposes in the modeling segment of the activity.

Skin Deep

Description

In the reading portions of many standardized tests, students must think about and interpret a character's personality, behavior, and motivations in relation to what happens in a passage. In this activity, students will consider characters from familiar stories and determine what they are most likely to do, say, think, or feel in different situations. Students will apply reasoning skills to their comprehension and interpretation of a given story. They will also put into practice their understanding of a particular character to specific contexts, determining what choices the character might make or behavior that seems the most realistic given the character's nature.

> ### Skills/State Standards
> ✗ Analyzing character

Materials You Need

- *Skin Deep* reproducible (page 90)
- Index cards
- Sample questions based on characters from the story (or stories) in specific situations
- Overhead projector and supplies

Getting Ready

Students should have read at least one story that includes a well-developed character or characters before tackling this activity. Characters from several stories could also be used simultaneously.

Select a character from a story to use as the basis for a series of questions about specific situations. The questions can be written in a multiple-choice format similar to the style and wording of those used on reading portions of your state's standardized test. The situations themselves can be varied in terms of the depth and detail, taking the lead from the types of characters used. For example, one type of situational question could be: "Which of these characters would most likely love french fries?" versus "Goldilocks walks into a shopping mall. Which of these events probably happened?" Some questions could even involve characters from different stories: "Little Red Riding Hood and Goldilocks have some similar qualities. What hobby might they share?"

Make a transparency of the questions and possible answers. Use the *Skin Deep* reproducible to make student handouts. If more than three characters will be involved in the game, make double-sided copies of the handout or as many as needed for students to complete.

Introducing the Activity

Lead students to recall the personality of a specific character from a story they know. Have them list some details about that character, for example, what he looks like or the choices he makes within the story. Next, ask students to think about what kind of car that character might drive, what his favorite food would be, or what he might do if he found a lost wallet on the sidewalk.

After they make a few hypotheses about the character in those situations, tell students that they just practiced an important skill—understanding and interpreting a character. Explain that they will use this skill every time they read a story, whether they are in the classroom or taking a standardized test. Tell students they will work in teams to determine the most reasonable choice, behavior, or outcome for a character within a specific situation outside of the original story.

Modeling the Activity

1. Using the transparency of situational questions, show students each question first while covering up the possible answers. Ask them to think about the character in that situation and propose answers from the original story in which the character appeared. Remind them to support their answer choice with proof from the story.

2. Show students the answer choices for each question and help them select the best answer for each given situation. Encourage them to explain why they chose that answer over the other choices.

3. Explain that students will use this same process when doing this activity on their teams.

Activity in Practice

1. Distribute copies of the *Skin Deep* handout to students to help them brainstorm about the characters before practicing the activity.

2. Divide the students into small teams and have them choose team names. Make a chart on the board or on an overhead transparency to keep track of the scores for each team.

3. Explain the process of the game:
   - A question will be read aloud and shown on an overhead transparency.
   - Each team will look at the answers, discuss which one makes the most sense in the situation, and write the team's choice on an index card.
   - Along with the answer, each team must also write down details or examples from the original story to support the team's answer choice for each question.
   - After all of the questions have been read and index cards collected, the questions are read aloud again with their correct answers. Teams receive a tally for each correct answer with valid textual support.

Extension

Students could use ideas from the questions about specific situations to create their own stories using the same characters in different settings and contexts.

Get Graphic!

Description

More and more standardized reading tests ask students to interpret and analyze information from a text represented in an alternative, graphic format. In this activity, students will create a text using the details in a completed graphic organizer. Through this process,

they will see how a selection can be structured graphically and learn how to apply this strategy to stories or other texts that they read.

Materials You Need

- *Get Graphic!* reproducibles (pages 91 and 92)
- Texts for modeling/practicing segments of activity (optional)
- Overhead projector and supplies

Getting Ready

This activity can be done either with authentic texts or details you create and complete on the organizer before distributing to students. If using actual texts, consider having students read the original texts after completing the activity, comparing and contrasting the versions they created with the actual ones.

Use one of the *Get Graphic!* reproducibles as a guideline for creating a completed graphic organizer. The type of text and its supporting details should dictate the style of graphic organizer you choose. You may need to create an organizer specifically to match a text used for the practice segment of the activity if one of the provided organizers does not work. Make a transparency and student handouts using the *Get Graphic!* reproducible that you have completed.

Introducing the Activity

Ask students to think of a familiar character from a recently read or well-known story. Discuss all the important aspects of the character—physical features, personality and attitude, likes/dislikes, strengths/weaknesses. Then ask students how they would organize all of that information. Would they make a list? Create a chart? Use a graphic organizer?

Remind students that graphic organizers are great tools for sorting out their thoughts and ideas. Tell students that they will practice using a graphic organizer but in a reverse way—instead of filling one in with all the details from a text, they will look at a completed graphic organizer, and use those details to create their own stories. Later, when they read a story, they can draw upon what they learned about the organization of details to complete a graphic organizer on their own.

Modeling the Activity

1. Review the different types of graphic organizers and their purposes. For example, what is the difference between a cause-and-effect graphic organizer and a story elements graphic organizer? Review what types of organizers are appropriate for different texts.

2. If students are not familiar with using graphic organizers, use the overhead projector to show them some forms suitable for texts they've read recently. As they recall different details and elements, ask students to help you complete one or two organizers.

3. Show students a completed graphic organizer sample (using one of the *Get Graphic!* handouts or another form) for either a story they have not read or one based on your own ideas. As you go over the different parts of the organizer, ask students how those details might work together to form a story or narrative of some kind.

4. Using an overhead transparency, jot down ideas for a rough outline of a story based on the details from the sample organizer.

5. Tell students that they will now form writing teams to create their own stories using the details from a completed graphic organizer.

Activity in Practice

1. Divide students into teams and distribute copies of a completed *Get Graphic!* handout or other organizer.

2. Tell students they will work together to combine the details into a story. Emphasize any elements you would like included in the story and give them to students as a guideline. They will brainstorm ideas, write them down, and begin drafting. Remind them that their stories must include all of the details in some way.

3. Once students have drafted their stories, have them write final versions and practice reading them aloud. Emphasize that everyone on each team should help present the story, whether reading dialogue or narration, acting out scenes, or—as the final portion of the team's presentation—explaining how all of the details fit into the story.

4. Have teams share their stories. Encourage creativity in their presentations. Allow teams time to explain how they incorporated all of the organizer's details.

5. After all the teams have shared, discuss any important details on the organizer that students did not see or make clear in their stories.

6. If time allows, ask students to read a story or other text in their teams. Then have them use details from the text to create an original graphic organizer.

Extension

You can adapt the activity to help students organize details from expository texts by creating categories before reading. After they have read the text, students can look back at the organizer and fill in the parts of the organizer with details from the text.

What Am I?

Description

In this activity, students will "meet" different genres as a variety of texts are transformed from static types of writing into lively quiz-show answer statements. The students become contestants who are presented with definitions, examples, and other characteristics of these types of writing. As contestants, they must figure out what belongs to each genre, offering a question as the response. Students gain active exposure to several genres at once while reinforcing their comprehension of the differences and significant features of each. Understanding these differences can help students see how texts are organized, understand the author's purpose, and look for features that make each genre unique.

> ### Skills/State Standards
> X Understanding genres
> X Comparison and contrast

Materials You Need:

- *What Am I?* reproducible (page 93)
- Texts for modeling and practice segments of activity
- Series of answer statements based on genre elements and text excerpts for practice segment
- Overhead projector and supplies

Getting Ready

The level of comprehension and skill of the students will determine the progression of answers and the range of genres to include. The first round could consist of simple personified statements, such as "I can rhyme" or "I usually have at least one character." The next round might include excerpts from actual texts that students have already read; they must identify the source of each excerpt as well as the genre of that source. The third round is the most challenging, as students identify the genre for excerpts from unfamiliar texts.

The types of answer statements for the first round should come from the most common features and elements of each genre. You may wish to review these features/elements with students before practicing the activity by using the *What Am I?* handout with students. The types of texts on the handout are intentionally left blank so that you can focus on the specific genres addressed on your state's standardized test. Use the *What Am I?* reproducible to create student handouts. Make an additional copy on a transparency to use during the modeling segment.

Introducing the Activity

Ask students to think about poetry. If a poem walked into the classroom, what would it look like? What if a fairy tale sat down at a nearby desk or a newspaper started talking? What makes each one of these types of writing—or genres—different from or the same as one another? What about the unique "personalities" of each?

Tell students that in this activity, they will get to "meet" these genres rather than simply reading them on the page. Explain that in a quiz-show format, students will identify the genre on the basis of important details, elements, and even actual excerpts. As the quiz show continues, the answer statements they encounter will grow more challenging. Explain that the purpose of the game is to have fun while figuring out and reviewing the different qualities of each genre.

Modeling the Activity

1. Distribute copies of the *What Am I?* handout to students. Using an overhead transparency of the reproducible, work with students to review the different elements and features of each genre.

2. Explain that when playing the game, the answer statement will be read first. Then, when student contestants are called on to respond, they should give their answers in the form of questions, such as "What is poetry?"

3. Offer the three types of answer statements that students will encounter in the activity. Read each answer statement aloud and ask students to write their responses on the back of their handouts. Then randomly call on a student to share the answer or ask for a volunteer.

4. After discussing the three different types of answer statements, tell students to review their completed handouts and refer to them while playing the game.

Activity in Practice

1. Decide how to structure the activity. Examples include:

   Structure A: Divide the class into two teams, and have each team send one player at a time to respond to an answer statement.

   Structure B: Divide the class into small teams. As each answer statement is read, ask each team to write its response on a card. Collect the cards at the end of each round, read the correct answers, and keep a tally of correct responses for each team.

2. After the activity, have students look again at their completed handouts and note any additional details they think are important. Tell them to use the handout as a reference when reading different types of texts on their own.

Extension

For further practice, students can use their ideas from the completed *What Am I?* handout to write a series of their own texts with a similar theme, but using the characteristics of each genre.

What's in the Bag?

Directions: In the chart below, write down the elements of the story or book you read. List your ideas for objects that you could use to create your brown bag for the story.

Story or Book Title: _____

Name of Your Story Bag: _____

Story Elements	Ideas for Objects
Setting *Place:* *Time:*	
Characters 1. 2. 3.	
Beginning of Story	
Middle of Story *Any Problems?*	
Ending of Story *Problems Solved?*	
Other Things You Liked:	

Compact Disc Artists

Name of Story/Text: _____

Step 1: Identify supporting details. Read through the story or text, looking for supporting details. Record the details you find in the compact disc shown below.

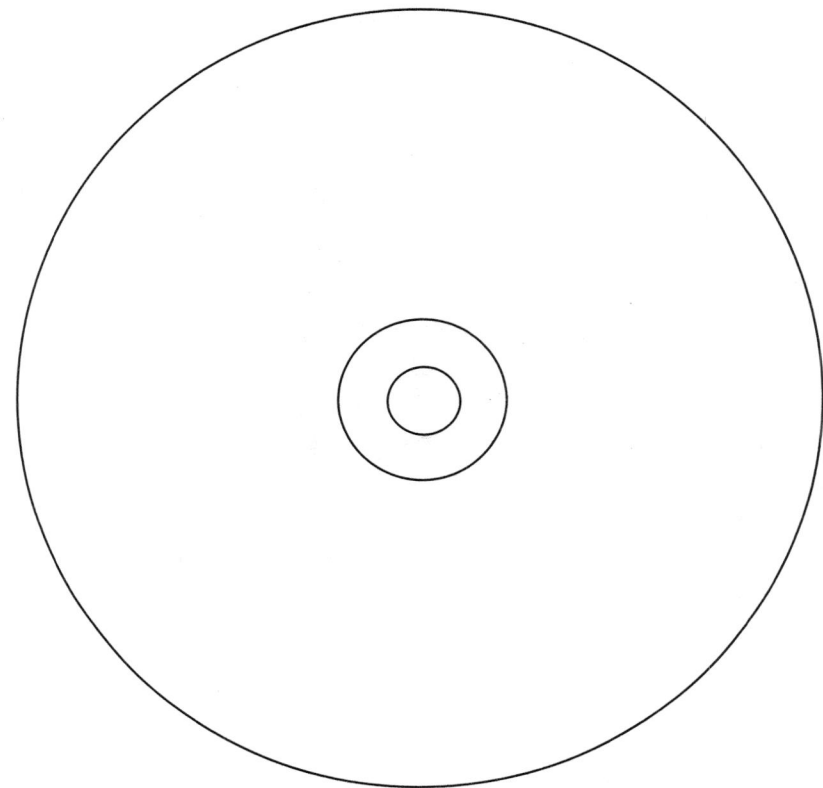

Step 2: Determine the main idea. Look at the details you wrote above in the compact disc. Then think about those details and write what you think the main idea is for the story or text.

_____

_____

Step 3: Share your ideas with the rest of your team. Use a separate sheet of paper to enter a title for your CD that is based on the main idea of the story or text. Write five to ten song titles based on the supporting details.

Name: Date:

Campfire Songs

Title of Story/Text: ___________________________________

Your Own Summary of the Story/Text:

Song Pattern to Use:

Write the words to the song you are using as a pattern for your own campfire song.

Your Campfire Song Version:

Hot Off the Press!

Directions: Complete this sheet to help plan a newspaper article based on your team's story.

Part 1: Information from the Story

Story Title: _____

Setting:

Characters:

_____   _____

_____   _____

Problem(s) in the Story:

Events Related to Problem(s) in the Story

Event 1: _____

Event 2: _____

Event 3: _____

Event 4: _____

Solution(s) in the Story:

Part 2: Planning Your Newspaper Article

Work with your team members to complete the next parts of this handout.
Complete the five Ws & H using information about the story.

Who: _____   When: _____

What: _____   Why: _____

Where: _____   How: _____

Now draft your newspaper article on a separate sheet of paper. Remember to include all essential details. Start with a good "lead," follow the style of a newspaper article (objective, fact-based, and including quotations from those involved in what happened), and come up with a headline and any "photographs" for your article.

Create a final version of your team's newspaper article using a poster board and art supplies.

Advertising Techniques

Avant garde—Using this item places the user ahead of the times.
  Example: "Kikoma. The car of tomorrow, today."

Bandwagon—Everybody is using it/doing it—so should you!
  Example: "Don't be left in the dust. Buy a Wrad Dirt Bike and ride with the pack!"

Facts and Figures—Objective information and statistics are used to prove superiority of item
  Example: "*Consumer Reports* rates the AquaSpritzer the quietest dishwasher."

Glittering Generalities—Positive words are used to suggest positive meaning about something
          with no real connection.
  Example: "Fun. Fresh. Fantastic. Flip Sportswear."

Hidden Fears—Use of the item protects you from your own hidden fears (embarrassment).
  Example: "Stop worrying about bad breath. Get Alaska Mints."

Magic Ingredients—This item contains a special ingredient that makes it better than its competition.
  Example: "Mega-Q. Only Sportsade power drinks have it."

Patriotism—By buying or using this, you show your patriotism.
  Example: "Our products are proudly made in the U.S.A."

Plain Folks—This item appeals to common, everyday people and is good enough for them.
  Example: "Country Diner. Nothing fancy, just good food and good people."

Snob Appeal—If you use this, you're part of the "in crowd."
  Example: "Big Britches. What world class skaters wear."

Testimonial—A famous or well-known person recommends an item.
  Example: "Get the hair product . . . uses. Rugby Hair Paste."

Transfer Words and Ideas—Positive connotations suggest positive qualities of the product.
  Example: Advertisement shows kid having fun with friends and drinking Cool-Cola,
          then cuts to shot of kid making a basket in a basketball game, and later leaving
          the game with parents drinking Cool-Cola. Announcer: "Cool-Cola makes
          good times even better."

Wit and Humor—Jokes, sight gags, and other funny visuals are used to entertain the audience
          with humor and which in turn attract them to the product or item.
  Example: Kid walking out of school with headphones on, singing loudly and badly.
          "TuneSpot MP3 players. Make some noise."

Target: Audience!

Directions: Use this sheet to help plan your print advertisement.

Title of Text: _____

1. What is the author's purpose for writing this text? Circle one of the purposes below:

   inform   persuade   entertain   express

2. Circle words or sentences from the text that helped you figure out its purpose. Look at what you circled and use the space below to explain the purpose of the text.

3. What type of advertising technique would work well with your team's text?

   _____

Complete the following chart with ideas for your team's advertisement.

Important Words from the Text to Include:	Any Pictures or Images to Use:	Title for Advertisement:

4. On the back of this sheet, sketch how your team's advertisement might look. Then share your ideas with your teammates and work together to create a final version of an advertisement for your team's text.

Skin Deep

Directions: Complete this chart for each character using the details from the story.

Character's name:	Character's name:	Character's name:
Physical description:	Physical description:	Physical description:
Things character does in story:	Things character does in story:	Things character does in story:
Emotions character has in story:	Emotions character has in story:	Emotions character has in story:
Big decisions character makes in story:	Big decisions character makes in story:	Big decisions character makes in story:
Other details about the character:	Other details about the character:	Other details about the character:

Get Graphic!

Focus: Character

Event		Event

Character

Event		Event

Get Graphic!

Focus: Story Web

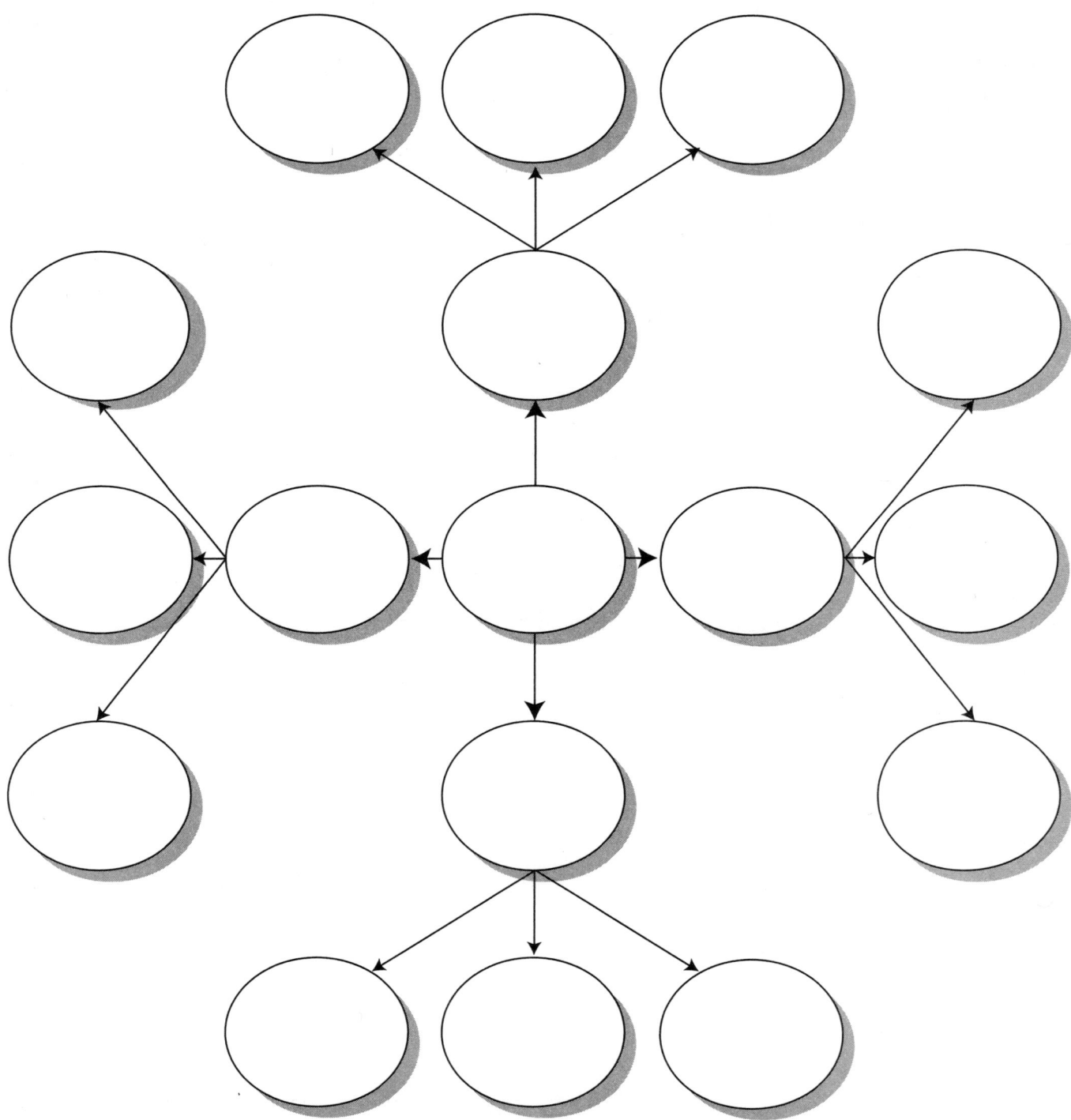

Name: **Date:**

What Am I?

Directions: Complete the following chart using details for each type of text.

Type of Text	Type of Text	Type of Text	Type of Text

Practice Reading Test—Grade 5

Name: _____

Date: _____ Class: _____

Directions: This test contains 4 reading selections and 31 questions. Read each selection. Then answer the questions. Mark your answers on your answer sheet. Be sure to fill in each bubble completely and erase any stray marks. Use the lines on the answer sheet to write each short-answer response. If you do not understand a question, ask your teacher for help.

Sample   What is the BEST antonym for the word **expensive**?

    A   limited

    B   pricey

    C   rich

    D   cheap   **Answers:**   (A) (B) (C) ●D

Note to Teacher: This chapter contains a reproducible practice test with the most common reading standards tested nationwide at the fifth-grade level. This test can be administered to your students before, during, or after they complete the activities in Chapter 5. (For a short diagnostic test, see Chapter 3.)

Practice Reading Test—Grade 5

Directions: Read the article. Then, answer questions 1 through 11 on your answer sheet.

Lassoing Big Ice

(1) Imagine this: Far out in the North Atlantic Ocean, a wayward 250,000-ton iceberg is floating along, slowly and quietly. It hasn't collided with anything—yet. But it's headed straight for a giant offshore oil platform, where hundreds of people live and work. The platform is stationary. The iceberg is moving. Can the giant iceberg be stopped? Would you know what to do? Well, Jerome Baker knows what to do, and he does it for a living. He is an "iceberg wrangler."

(2) Baker helps keep icebergs from colliding with the Hibernia oil platform, which lies almost 200 miles off the coast of Newfoundland. This platform drills for oil in 250 feet of water. The platform is huge and sturdy, and it's protected by an underwater belt made of giant concrete teeth. But who knows what damage a half-million ton iceberg might do? It's Baker's job to keep the platform and the icebergs from meeting, and to keep himself and his crew safe while he's doing it.

(3) All year long, Baker and his crew on his ship, the *Norseman*, are busy delivering food and supplies to the workers on the platform. But the busiest time for Baker and his crew is from February through July. During those warmer months, icebergs break away and start to drift down into "iceberg alley," off the coast of Newfoundland near the Hibernia platform.

(4) To help spot these roving ice chunks, a local airline company keeps a lookout for big icebergs as well as little ones, which are called "bergy bits." When they see something, people from the airline call Baker on his boat radio. Then, Baker decides on the best way to deal with the iceberg, big or small.

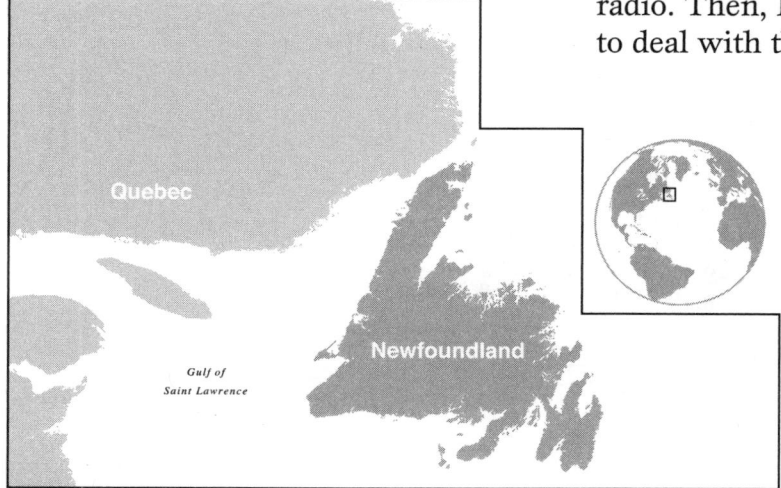

Quebec

Gulf of Saint Lawrence

Newfoundland

GO ON ➡

(5) How do Baker and his crew stop an iceberg? That depends on the iceberg's size. For bergy bits, Baker can back up his ship and use the propeller's movement to push the berg into a current where it can float harmlessly away. Dealing with icebergs that weigh tens of thousands of tons can be a bit more challenging. An iceberg can be the length of two football fields and rise as high as 240 feet out of the water. Using towropes that are up to 1,200 feet long, Baker wrangles a giant iceberg by lassoing it. He wraps the rope around the berg like a belt, adds a wire towline that's connected to the *Norseman*, then pulls the berg away from the oil platform.

(6) But some lassoed icebergs have minds of their own. They might slip out of the ropes, turn over, or even break up into smaller chunks that could cause more damage. A flipped iceberg may have jagged bottom edges that get tangled in the ropes, or it may cause huge waves when it flips. Baker maintains a safe distance, keeping at least one and one-half miles between the *Norseman* and the berg. Because towing an iceberg is tricky, Baker and his crew might spend up to three days wrangling just one berg!

(7) During his 20 years on the job, Baker has seen other ideas for wrangling icebergs come and go. In the 1960s, the U.S. Coast Guard thought they could melt icebergs by spreading carbon black on them, like frosting a cupcake. As the black coating absorbed the sunlight, the ice was supposed to melt—most of the bergs just flipped over instead. In the 1980s, Baker tried to push the bergs away by shooting a water cannon at them. It worked for the bergy bits, but not the big bergs. Another crew tried using a remote-controlled vehicle to drill holes into the bergs and put towlines in them. Unfortunately, the seas were too choppy for this idea to work.

(8) Despite the unpredictable nature of his job, Baker finds it interesting and worthwhile. This cowboy of the sea wouldn't trade his job for anything else. Whether it's a bergy bit or a 250,000-ton monster, Baker says wrangling icebergs is all in a day's work.

GO ON ⟹

1 How does Baker find out about icebergs headed for the oil platform?

   A He sees them in the distance.

   B He gets a call on his boat radio.

   C He spots them from an airplane overhead.

   D He watches for them from the platform.

2 To move an iceberg, Baker most often—

   F uses a water cannon to push it away.

   G drills holes and inserts wires into it.

   H ties a huge rope around it.

   J coats the surface with carbon black.

3 Read this sentence from the article.

   Baker helps keep icebergs from colliding with the Hibernia oil platform, which lies almost 200 miles off the coast of Newfoundland.

   Which word has almost the same meaning as **colliding**?

   A damaging

   B merging

   C fighting

   D smashing

4 What was the author's purpose in writing this article?

   F to teach readers how to wrangle an iceberg

   G to encourage others to try Baker's job

   H to describe the work involved in an unusual job

   J to inform readers about icebergs

5 If the article needed a new title, which would be the BEST choice?

   A "Ice Cowboy"

   B "North Atlantic Icebergs"

   C "Floating Cubes of Trouble"

   D "Jerome Baker's Job"

6 Which is the most likely meaning of the word **roving** as used in paragraph 4?

   F tracking

   G moving aimlessly

   H trapped

   J melting

GO ON ⇨

Practice Reading Test—Grade 5 (continued)

7 According to the article, how much do the icebergs that Baker tows weigh?

   A 1,200 pounds

   B about as much as several football players

   C tens of thousands of tons

   D over one million tons

8 Which of the following is NOT a fact stated in the article?

   F Icebergs vary in size.

   G Icebergs can flip over in the ocean.

   H Icebergs are found only in "iceberg alley."

   J A small iceberg chunk can cause damage.

9 In the last sentence of the article, what does the phrase "all in a day's work" mean?

   A enough work for just one day

   B a hard job

   C just a normal part of a job

   D a type of work that is done during the day

10 Which of the following is a reason the article gives in paragraph 6 for why Baker's boat must keep a distance of a mile and a half between his boat and an iceberg in tow?

   F If the iceberg flipped, it would create huge waves.

   G The iceberg could change direction and crash into the boat.

   H The boat can tow the iceberg faster at this distance.

   J The crew has a better view of other icebergs.

11 SHORT ANSWER: Answer the following question on your answer sheet. Use complete sentences.

In your own words, describe methods other than towing that have been used to stop icebergs from hitting the Hibernia oil platform. Why didn't they work as well?

Practice Reading Test—Grade 5 (continued)

Directions: Read the story. Then, answer questions 12 through 18 on your answer sheet.

The Three Brothers

(1) In a faraway land, three brothers were known for telling tall tales that no one ever believed. They enjoyed going from place to place, telling their stories to willing listeners. The brothers told their stories as if they were true, knowing they were not. After hearing their far-fetched, impossible tales, people would often doubt their truthfulness, claiming that the stories were unbelievable and false.

(2) On one of their journeys far away from home, the three brothers came upon a wealthy prince traveling alone. The prince was dressed in beautiful clothes and wore many exquisite jewels that were both rare and strange. The three brothers saw the prince's possessions and wanted them. They imagined themselves as wealthy lords in fine clothing. So they decided to use their gift for storytelling to trick the prince into giving them his possessions.

(3) The next day, the oldest brother told the prince, "We have many great stories to share with you, dear prince. We are sure you have many fine tales to tell as well. We should tell each other our stories, and if any of us doubts the truth of what he hears, that doubting person must become a servant to him who tells the story." This may seem like a strange way for the brothers to gain the prince's riches, since they did not need a servant. However, if the prince doubted their tales, he would become their servant. Then the brothers would be able to take his possessions and make them their own.

(4) The prince was amused and agreed to the contest. Since everyone always gasped with disbelief after hearing their stories, the brothers were sure they would win. To make the contest fair, they found a villager nearby and asked him to be the judge. Then, they all sat down under a shady tree and began to tell stories.

GO ON →

(5)   The youngest brother was the first to tell a tale. Grinning from ear to ear, he started, "When I was very young, I saw a large tree and wanted to climb it and hide from my brothers. I stayed in the highest part of the tree all day long while my brothers went everywhere trying to find me. Once the sun went down, my brothers went home. But I was so high up, I couldn't climb down the tree by myself. I knew I needed a rope to help me, so I went to a nearby shed, found a long rope, and used it to climb down the tree and go home."

(6)   When the youngest brother was done, the prince sat quietly, not saying a word. The brothers were surprised, but decided to continue with their plan. The second brother then began his story, hoping that his tale would be so ridiculous that the prince would have to burst out with disbelief. He said, "When my brother was hiding from us that same day, we searched for him everywhere. I looked deep in the forest. Suddenly, I saw something move and dart into a cave. I thought it was my brother, so I chased it. I soon discovered that it was not my brother, but a ferocious tiger.

(7)   "The tiger was hungry and opened his mouth to eat me up. But I outsmarted him— instead of letting him eat me, I jumped into his mouth and slid down to his belly before he could take one bite. Then I made such a fuss inside of him, screaming and jumping around, that the tiger was afraid and confused. He spit me out so powerfully that I shot like a cannonball into the air and back to my village, landing in a haystack. The tiger was so frightened that he decided not to come anywhere near our village. I went looking for my brother and instead saved our village from a huge tiger."

(8)   When the second brother was done, he waited with wide eyes to hear what the prince would say. The prince sat quietly and said nothing, so the oldest brother started his tale. Even though the three brothers were upset and angry, they decided that the prince could not remain quiet after hearing the next story.

(9)   The oldest brother stood up and said, "One afternoon I was walking along the riverbank near our village. All the fishermen I met were very unhappy. I asked them what was making them so sad. Each one told me that they had not caught a single fish for a week. No fish meant no money or food for their families. So I decided to help them. I dove into the river and changed into a fish. I swam upstream and searched for the fish. That is when I saw what had happened. A giant fish was eating all of the smaller fish before they swam downstream. When the giant fish saw me, he swam over to eat me, too. But I outsmarted him. I changed back into myself and drew my large sword. As the giant fish came near, I sliced his belly wide open. All of the fish inside swam out and down to the fishermen's nets."

(10) When the oldest brother finished his story, all three brothers looked at the prince, wondering what he was going to say. The prince acted like he believed the story. This shocked the brothers. They were very angry, but waited for the prince to tell his story. Their plan was to believe the prince's story, no matter what he said.

(11) The prince took his turn, and began to tell his tale: "I am a wealthy prince with many possessions. I have been traveling through the land in search of three servants who ran away from my castle. I have searched for them for many months. I was just about to give up looking for them until I met you three men. Now, my search is over, because I have found my missing servants. You three brothers are the servants who ran away from my castle."

(12) After the prince finished his tale, the brothers were speechless. They were caught in their own trick. If they said the story was false, they would have to become the prince's servants. If they said the story was true, they would be admitting that they were the runaway servants. The villager acting as the judge decided that the prince had won the contest.

(13) Instead of making the three brothers return with him to his castle, the prince allowed them to go back to their own village. Before he let them go, he made the three brothers promise to never tell a tall tale again. From that day on, the brothers became known far and wide for being honest and truthful.

12 What is the most logical meaning of the word **far-fetched** in paragraph 1?

A exotic

B unlikely

C long

D funny

13 Why do the three brothers want to have a contest with the prince?

F They want to become his servants.

G They want to go to his castle.

H They want his jewels and clothes.

J They want to entertain him with stories.

14 The brothers in this story can BEST be described as—

A clever.

B foolish.

C wise.

D innocent.

GO ON

Practice Reading Test—Grade 5 (continued)

15 What happens RIGHT AFTER the second brother tells his story?

F The oldest brother begins his story.

G The prince starts to object.

H The judge declares the prince the winner.

J The prince asks the oldest brother to start.

16 The author probably wrote this story to—

A explain why the prince doesn't have any servants.

B remind others about the importance of being honest.

C show how lucky princes are in comparison to villagers.

D tell a true story about people in the past.

17 This story can BEST be described as—

F a fable.

G a fairy tale.

H a factual article.

J a science fiction story.

18 Look at this web about the prince.

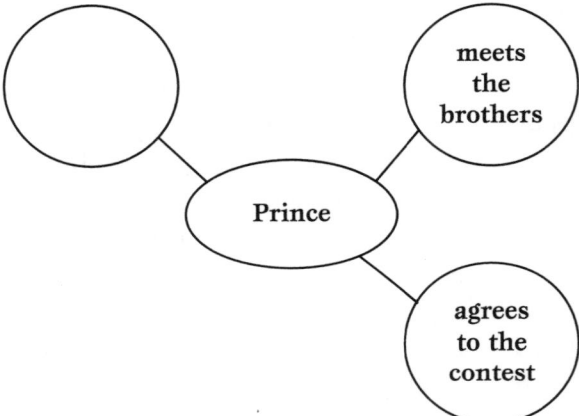

Which phrase BEST fits in the empty circle of the web?

A takes the brothers as servants

B sells his castle

C gives away his jewels

D outsmarts the brothers

GO ON ➡

Directions: Read the poem. Then, answer questions 19 through 24 on your answer sheet.

The Moon
by Robert Louis Stevenson

1   The moon has a face like the clock in the hall;
2   She shines on thieves on the garden wall,
3   On streets and fields and harbour quays,
4   And birdies asleep in the forks of the trees.

5   The squalling cat and the squeaking mouse,
6   The howling dog by the door of the house,
7   The bat that lies in bed at noon,
8   All love to be out by the light of the moon.

9   But all of the things that belong to the day
10   Cuddle to sleep to be out of her way;
11   And flowers and children close their eyes
12   Till up in the morning the sun shall arise.

GO ON ➜

Practice Reading Test—Grade 5 (continued)

19 The main idea of this poem is to—

F explain how the moon affects animals.

G describe the moon's special qualities and things that occur at night.

H describe how the moon is better than the sun.

J explain why humans can't live under the moon.

20 According to the poem, what comes out under the moonlight?

A birds

B children

C bats

D flowers

21 Which line from the poem gives human qualities to something that is NOT human?

F "The moon has a face like the clock in the hall"

G "The bat that lies in bed at noon"

H "And birdies asleep in the forks of the trees"

J "The howling dog by the door of the house"

22 You can tell that the speaker in the poem—

A thinks the moon is interesting.

B is scared of what happens at night.

C wishes the moon were like the sun.

D wants to be like the moon.

23 Which line from the poem makes a comparison between two things?

F "The moon has a face like the clock in the hall"

G "The bat that lies in bed at noon"

H "Cuddle to sleep to be out of her way"

J "She shines on thieves on the garden wall"

24 Why does the author say that the moon "shines on thieves on the garden wall"?

A to show that the moon can cast shadows like the sun

B because thieves are most likely to be out at night

C to remind the reader that thieves can climb walls

D to show how pretty nighttime events can be

GO ON

Directions: Read the experiment. Then, answer questions 25 through 31 on your answer sheet.

How to Build a Hovercraft

(1) Hovercrafts are vehicles that travel just above the ground or the water. A cushion of air keeps them from touching the surface. They can go just as fast as cars or motorboats. They use less fuel because there is no friction to slow them down.

(2) Try building your own hovercraft! This one will only be big enough for a mouse to ride, but it's a start! You will need: a piece of cardboard, a balloon, some glue, a thread spool, a pencil, and scissors. And don't forget your passenger!

(3) Start by cutting the cardboard into a four-inch square. Then use a pencil to punch a hole in the middle of it. Get an adult to help you, or be very careful with the scissors! The hole should be as big as the hole in the spool.

(4) Next, glue the spool onto the cardboard so the holes line up. Before the glue dries, use a pencil to line up the hole in the cardboard with the hole in the spool. Make sure there is no extra glue stopping up the hole.

(5) Stretch the balloon over the top of the spool. Now blow through the hole in the cardboard to inflate the balloon. It is the air from the balloon that will power the hovercraft. Pinch it closed so the air doesn't come out.

(6) Put your hovercraft on a smooth, flat surface like a table. Get your passenger settled onto the cardboard—we're about ready to lift off! When you let go of the balloon, your hovercraft should glide across the table. Try pushing it a little.

25 Which is the best way to combine these sentences in paragraph 1?

They can go just as fast as cars or motorboats.

They use less fuel because there is no friction to slow them down.

F They can go just as fast as cars or motorboats so they use less fuel because there is no friction to slow them down.

G They can go just as fast as cars or motorboats since they use less fuel because there is no friction to slow them down.

H They can go just as fast as cars or motorboats, because they use less fuel because there is no friction to slow them down.

J They can go just as fast as cars or motorboats but they use less fuel because there is no friction to slow them down.

26 Which of the following meanings of the word **stop** is used in paragraph 4?

A to close by filling or obstructing

B to cause to give up or change course of action

C to cease an activity or operation; to come to an end, especially suddenly

D to arrest the progress or motion of

27 Why do you think the instructions tell you to make sure that there is no glue stopping up the hole?

F so the hovercraft looks good

G so the hovercraft weighs less

H so the balloon won't stick to the extra glue

J so the air can travel all the way from the balloon to beneath the cardboard

GO ON ➡

Practice Reading Test—Grade 5 (continued)

28 Which of the following sentences from the passage is not part of the instructions on how to build a hovercraft?

A Stretch the balloon over the top of the spool.

B Try building your own hovercraft!

C Start by cutting the cardboard into a four-inch square.

D Next, glue the spool onto the cardboard so the holes line up.

29 The purpose of this passage is to—

F show you how to save fuel.

G explain the dangers of using scissors without an adult present.

H teach you how to do a fun science project.

J show you that a hovercraft is not a good means of transportation.

30 Hovercraft is a compound word that comes from the words hover and craft. Considering what the passage teaches you about hovercraft, what is the most likely meaning of the word hover?

A to sit just above something

B to carry a single passenger

C to travel through water

D to travel over rocky terrain

31 SHORT ANSWER: Answer the following question on your answer sheet. Use complete sentences.

How does this hovercraft work?

END OF PRACTICE TEST

Practice Reading Test—Grade 5
Answer Sheet

Directions: Mark your answers on this answer sheet. Be sure to fill in each bubble completely and erase any stray marks. Use the lines provided to write each short-answer response.

1 Ⓐ Ⓑ Ⓒ Ⓓ

2 Ⓕ Ⓖ Ⓗ Ⓙ

3 Ⓐ Ⓑ Ⓒ Ⓓ

4 Ⓕ Ⓖ Ⓗ Ⓙ

5 Ⓐ Ⓑ Ⓒ Ⓓ

6 Ⓕ Ⓖ Ⓗ Ⓙ

7 Ⓐ Ⓑ Ⓒ Ⓓ

8 Ⓕ Ⓖ Ⓗ Ⓙ

9 Ⓐ Ⓑ Ⓒ Ⓓ

10 Ⓕ Ⓖ Ⓗ Ⓙ

11 SHORT ANSWER: On the lines below, please answer the following question in complete sentences.

In your own words, describe methods other than towing that have been used to stop icebergs from hitting the Hibernia oil platform. Why didn't they work as well?

_____

_____

_____

_____

_____

12 Ⓐ Ⓑ Ⓒ Ⓓ

13 Ⓕ Ⓖ Ⓗ Ⓙ

14 Ⓐ Ⓑ Ⓒ Ⓓ

15 Ⓕ Ⓖ Ⓗ Ⓙ

16 Ⓐ Ⓑ Ⓒ Ⓓ

17 Ⓕ Ⓖ Ⓗ Ⓙ

18 Ⓐ Ⓑ Ⓒ Ⓓ

19 Ⓕ Ⓖ Ⓗ Ⓙ

20 Ⓐ Ⓑ Ⓒ Ⓓ

21 Ⓕ Ⓖ Ⓗ Ⓙ

Practice Reading Test—Grade 5 (continued)

Answer Sheet

22 (A) (B) (C) (D)

23 (F) (G) (H) (J)

24 (A) (B) (C) (D)

25 (F) (G) (H) (J)

26 (A) (B) (C) (D)

27 (F) (G) (H) (J)

28 (A) (B) (C) (D)

29 (F) (G) (H) (J)

30 (A) (B) (C) (D)

31 SHORT ANSWER: On the lines below, please write your answer in complete sentences.

How does this hovercraft work?

_____

_____

_____

_____

_____

_____

 **Skill-Building Math Activities**

This chapter includes 11 different activities designed to help you build and reinforce students' mathematical skills. Each activity provides an engaging way for students to practice one or more key skills that will be assessed on your state's standardized tests. Students will be asked to use their knowledge, experiences, and imaginations while strengthening their abilities to use math more frequently and fluidly. Each activity is structured in the following format:

✗ Skills/State Standards—breakdown of the skills addressed in the activity

✗ Description—brief summary of the activity

✗ Materials You Need—list of materials required for the activity

✗ Getting Ready—tips for the teacher and a description of what to do in order to prepare for the activity

✗ Introducing the Activity—suggestions for introducing the activity and capturing students' interest

✗ Modeling the Activity—ideas for demonstrating the activity (if applicable)

✗ Activity in Practice—step-by-step instructions for working through the activity

✗ Extensions—variations, extensions, and other teaching suggestions

All of the activities are designed to be hands-on and team-oriented, requiring active participation by your students. They are also flexible in nature and can be modified to meet your students' needs, as well as give students individual practice. You can use the activities in any order. You may find that some are more suited to the particular needs of your students than others.

Some activities also include reproducible pages. These pages are found at the end of this chapter, beginning on page 134.

The matrix on page 111 organizes the activities by the predominant skills or standards they address. Some activities address more than one skill and may, therefore, appear under more than one category on the chart.

Matrix of Skills Addressed in Math Activities

Skill/State Standard	Activity	Page
Numbers and operations	Time Flies	112
	Marketplace Mayhem	114
	Classified Careers	116
	Money Madness	118
Place value	Money Madness	118
Patterns and relationships	Mathematales	120
	Pattern Puzzles	122
Algebraic thinking	Classified Careers	116
	Mathematales	120
	Pattern Puzzles	122
Geometry and spatial reasoning	Geo Road Trip	124
	Amusement Architects	126
Measurement	Geo Road Trip	124
	Amusement Architects	126
	You Rule!	128
Probability and statistics	Wacky Stats	130
Mathematical processes and problem solving	Marketplace Mayhem	114
	You Rule!	128
	No Problem	132
Working with fractions, decimals, and percentages	Time Flies	112
Estimating and rounding	Time Flies	112
Graphing	Time Flies	112
	Classified Careers	116
	Wacky Stats	130
Analyzing data	Time Flies	112

Time Flies

Description

Examining how students spend their time each day is one way to incorporate basic numerical operations in a real-life context. In this activity, students make predictions and estimations about how they spend their time. Then they keep a daily log for one week, recording how they actually do spend their time. Using the resulting data, students then calculate the time breakdowns for each category and represent them in different ways—fractions, percentages, and displays of

<table>
<tr><td>

Skills/State Standards

✗ Numbers and operations

✗ Working with fractions, decimals, and percentages

✗ Estimating and rounding

✗ Graphing

✗ Analyzing data

</td></tr>
</table>

results in a pie chart. After comparing their completed charts with their initial estimations, students then compare their time charts with each other by each creating a bar graph representing how the class spends its time as a whole.

Materials You Need

- *Time Flies* reproducible (page 134)
- *Weekly Log* reproducible (page 135)
- Sample time log and chart/graph for modeling activity
- Overhead projector and supplies

Getting Ready

Use a weekly log based on your own time schedule for modeling this activity.

Make student handouts using *Time Flies* and *Weekly Log* reproducibles.

Introducing the Activity

Ask students to think about this fact: According to the Department of Education, children in the United States watch an average of three to five hours of television every day. Ask them if that is true for them. How else do they spend their time each day?

Next, ask students to guess what percentage of time they spend sleeping every day. If they sleep an average of 8 hours a night, $^8/_{24}$ equals what percentage of the day?

Tell students that keeping track of their time is one way to help them manage their time better and to exercise their mathematical skills. Explain that in this activity they will keep a daily time log for one week and then use that information to figure out the fractional and percentage amounts of how they spend their time. They will make a pie chart to represent the data collected. All of this information is then combined to create a class graph or chart, showing how the entire class spends its time for an average day or week.

Modeling the Activity

1. Ask students to brainstorm different ways that people spend their time in an average day and develop categories together. Some possible categories are: school/work, sleeping, eating, hobbies, playing/recreation, doing chores, homework.

2. Using these categories and any others that apply to your sample, make estimations on how much time you spend per day doing each of these things.

3. Show students a sample estimated time log for one day, using the handout as a guide.

4. Convert the data for each category into fractional and percentage amounts.

5. Show students your pie chart based on the sample time log's percentages. Underneath the chart, compare your estimations with how you actually spent your time that day.

6. Encourage students to draw conclusions about how you spend your time. Do you spend too much time doing one thing instead of another? How could you balance your daily schedule to make time for things you like to do?

Activity in Practice

1. Distribute copies of the *Time Flies* handouts to students and have them estimate the total time amounts for each category, recording their estimates in Step 1.

2. Then distribute copies of the *Weekly Log* handouts and have students keep track of their time for one week using the same major categories.

3. After they complete their *Weekly Log* handout, have students use the times for each category to develop fractional and percentage amounts and record them in Step 3 on the *Time Flies* handout.

4. Next, have them create a pie chart to represent the data recorded.

5. Have students compare their pie charts and use them to develop a bar graph showing how the whole class spends its time in an average week.

Extension

Consider having different classes compete with each other to see which class has the highest time percentage for a particular category, such as reading, homework, community service or some other school-related activity.

Marketplace Mayhem

Description

In this activity, students will draw upon several mathematical processes and problem-solving skills within a simulated, real-world context. Working in teams, students will create products, determine target markets, and calculate associated costs and potential profits. The second phase of the activity is similar to a board game: each team must deal with a situation, problem, or event in the "marketplace" that has mathematical implications for the product. For example, a huge demand for a shrinking supply raises the price of the most essential item in a product, or a new tax is created for products made for a particular age group. Each team must determine how its product will fare in the marketplace.

Skills/State Standards
X Numbers and operations
X Mathematical processes and problem solving

Materials You Need

- *Marketplace Mayhem* reproducible (page 136)
- Sample products and product information
- Cards containing individual mathematical/economic situations or "Marketplace News Report"
- Overhead projector and supplies

Getting Ready

Having samples of real and imaginary products and specific information about their manufacturing and marketing will help students when completing the handout for this activity.

Decide whether each team will deal with the same or different marketplace events and situations. If each team is given the same event, the marketplace is more equal. Another option is to issue a "Marketplace News Report" containing several events at once. In this scenario, all teams would deal with one or more events that apply to their products. These situations or events could be geared toward the products that students have created or taken from current events in the news or financial marketplace. This activity will require research time to collect information about product materials, ingredients, and associated costs.

Make student handouts and a transparency for modeling the activity using the *Marketplace Mayhem* reproducible.

Introducing the Activity

Show students a familiar product. Ask them to tell you some basics about the product: what it is, who buys it, how much it costs, what it's made of, and who makes it. Then ask students to guess how much it costs to produce/manufacture the item and how much revenue or profit the company makes from it in one year. Compare their guesses with the real statistics. Tell students that lots of factors, or variables, go into how well a product succeeds, and those variables can affect some products more than others. For example, if a newly released health study stated that green beans are the best vegetable to eat, how would that affect the sales of a snack food called "Beanables" made from green beans? Or, if an entire crop of green beans was destroyed, how would that affect the amount of "Beanables" produced and sold?

Tell students that in this activity, they will act as entrepreneurs, developing, marketing, and selling their own products. After their businesses are established, they will have to decide how changes in the marketplace affect their production costs, rate, sales, and profits.

Modeling the Activity

1. Use the same product from the introduction, another familiar product, or an imaginary product you have created. Explain how you researched the information to complete each portion of the transparency of the *Market Mayhem* reproducible. Emphasize that you kept your product choice simple so that you could find the information you needed.

2. Brainstorm with students about what kinds of things could happen to increase sales of your product. Then ask students to offer ideas of "worst-case scenarios"—what might cause your product to lose money.

3. Read three examples of situations/events/problems to students and ask them how each might affect your product. Show students how to calculate the potential changes in production costs, sales, and profits for one month.

Activity in Practice

1. Divide the class into teams and distribute copies of the *Marketplace Mayhem* handout.

2. As teams complete the handout, they may need access to the Internet or the library to help them do the necessary research.

3. Once teams have completed the handout together, decide whether to issue a "Marketplace News Report" or have each team draw one or more cards with a separate situation/event.

4. After a round of cards/reports is issued, have each team figure out how their product is affected by making calculations and estimations based on the information.

5. Ask teams to give "monthly" or "annual" reports about their products' profits or losses.

Extensions

As an added feature, issue each student $10,000 in play money to invest in one of the products. Tell the students to develop an initial public offering, or IPO, for each product and then try to convince their fellow classmates to invest in their new products. Have each student keep track of her own investments. Award prizes or incentives to students who prove to be savvy investors.

Classified Careers

Description

This activity uses the newspaper to apply and develop a variety of math skills. Students first assume the role of a job hunter, scanning the classifieds for a job that interests them. Considering the salary or hourly wages, they determine a budget with housing/rent costs, food, and other monthly expenses using information from other sections of the

┌─────────────────────────────────┐
│ **Skills/State Standards**   │
│ **X** Numbers and operations   │
│ **X** Graphing   │
│ **X** Algebraic thinking   │
└─────────────────────────────────┘

newspaper, and, if necessary, from other print resources. Students then represent their budget in alternative forms, such as a chart or graph. They also may find other items in the paper that they'd like to purchase and, given their budgets, determine if those purchases are affordable or not.

Materials You Need

- *Classified Careers* reproducible (page 137)
- Several copies of the newspaper
- Sample career and budget for modeling activity
- Overhead projector and supplies

Getting Ready

Having several editions of the paper may be helpful so students have a wide variety of classifieds when selecting their careers.

If students have already completed a unit on careers, consider having students select a certain vocation and find wage information using career manuals instead of the classifieds.

Make student handouts using the *Classified Careers* reproducible. Also replicate an additional copy on a transparency to use during the modeling portion of the activity.

Introducing the Activity

Ask students what kinds of jobs they might like to try. Look at a section of the classifieds and read a few of the job openings, encouraging discussion about what each job might be like.

Tell students that although they have plenty of time to think about a potential career, they will get to apply some practical mathematical skills by selecting a job from the newspaper classifieds right now. Explain that using the salary or wage information and other information from the newspaper, they will create a monthly budget. Finally, they will choose things to buy, and determine if they can afford them—or if they need a different career!

Modeling the Activity

1. Display a transparency of the classified advertisement for the job you have chosen for the modeling activity. Read through the advertisement together and show students how to calculate what your monthly income would be, given the hourly wage or salary listed.

2. Ask students to name some monthly expenses: rent/housing, car payment, food, utilities, entertainment, purchases, etc. Then show students your budget in chart form. Explain how you figured out the costs and basic estimates for each category. Show students other parts of the newspaper, such as the car sales and rental ads, that you used to determine costs. Remind students that your income will determine how much you can afford in terms of housing and transportation.

3. Show students a graphical representation of your budget such as a pie chart or bar graph and lead them in a discussion on the process of creating graphs.

4. Generate a list of other items you might want to purchase. Considering your budget, invite students to help you figure out if you can afford those items or if you need to save your money to purchase them later. Research the costs of the items by using other parts of the newspaper.

5. Tell students that they will work in pairs when completing this activity. Each student will select a career from the classifieds, but they will share a place to live.

Activity in Practice

1. Divide the class into teams of two students and give each pair a newspaper and a copy of the *Classified Careers* handout.

2. As students select jobs from the newspaper, be available to assist them if there is no salary or wage listed for the position.

3. After the pairs have completed the handout, ask them to share their selected jobs and budgets with the class.

4. After each pair's presentation, have students share how this activity used their math skills in a practical way. Then ask them if this activity will affect the types of jobs they are interested in pursuing when they are ready to enter the world of work.

Extensions

This activity could be broadened or simplified depending on time constraints and needs. For example, students could be given a set amount of money to spend on a newspaper shopping spree. After selecting their items to "purchase," they would calculate the totals, including any relevant sales tax, and then explain why they selected those items.

Money Madness

Description

In this game-format activity, students work on their place-value skills while playing with imaginary money. Each team of students is given a large sum as their total net worth/spending money at the beginning of the game. In each game round, a money-related question is randomly posed to a team.

The questions are related to identifying place value and basic operations of large whole numbers and decimals. Each team that correctly answers a question receives a point. At the end of the game, the team with the most points—or money left—wins.

> ### *Skills/State Standards*
> ✗ Place value
> ✗ Numbers and operations

Materials You Need

- *Money Madness* reproducible (page 138)
- Index cards or overhead transparencies containing game questions
- Overhead projector and supplies

Getting Ready

The types of questions on the game cards can vary depending on the skills you want to target. If students need more practice with whole numbers in the billions, you may want to give them one billion instead of one million as the numerical starting point.

Some examples of questions are:
   "You just purchased a ski boat for $4,678. How much money do you have left?"
   "What is the place value of the number 6 in the cost of the ski boat?"
   "You invested in a stock that cost $5,000 a share. You bought 3 shares. Then the stock
      went up in value to $17,890. How much money did you make?"
   "What number is in the ten hundreds place after subtracting the cost of an ice cream store
      you bought for $17,875?"

You many also want to ask each team more questions that connect or build upon one another as the game continues with each round.

Make student handouts using the *Money Madness* reproducible. Make an additional copy on a transparency to use during the modeling portion of the activity. Use the reproducible to make a place-value mat ranging from the hundred billions down to the hundredths for each team. The handout includes space to answer five questions. If more space is needed, make additional copies or have students use the backs of their sheets.

Introducing the Activity

Ask students what they would do if they had a million dollars. How would they spend it? After students offer ideas, write out the number numerically and ask them to tell you the place value of the numeral 1. Explain the importance of knowing place value—it tells you the value of each digit, and that is helpful when you have a number as large as 1,000,000.

Tell students that in this activity each team will be given one million dollars. Explain how the game will work: a money-related question will be displayed on the overhead or read aloud. The question will relate to the place value of numbers as well as basic operations (addition, subtraction, multiplication, division).

Each team will work on the question and come up with an answer, but only one team, selected randomly, will give its answer. A team will be awarded one point for each correct answer. Explain that the object of the game is to answer each question correctly.

Modeling the Activity

1. Using an overhead transparency, write down the starting monetary sum for the game. Replicate the place-value mat from the *Money Madness* handout and show students how to label each place value of that number.

2. Under the amount, write down and read aloud two or more sample questions (see examples from the "Getting Ready" section). Show students how to do the calculations.

Activity in Practice

1. Divide the class into small teams and distribute copies of the *Money Madness* handout.

2. Explain the game procedures:
   - Each team will be given the same monetary sum at the beginning of the game.
   - A question is asked, and a short amount of time will be given to work out an answer.
   - A team will be randomly chosen to share an answer. If the team answers correctly, it will receive a point. All teams will need to "correct" any wrong answers before the next question so all begin with the same number for each round.

3. Use the overhead to show students each question visually, or use index cards to select a question for each round.

4. Each team should be asked the same total number of questions so that each team gets an equal chance to make the same number of points.

5. Create questions that will be open for any team to answer to serve as a tie-breaker.

Extension

This game can be altered and played within small teams. Each member of the team could be given the same sum but draw different cards for each round; at the end of the game, the member with the most money remaining is the winner.

Mathematales

Description

Understanding patterns and recognizing numerical relationships are fundamental components of basic algebra. In this activity, students will use their linguistic and creative abilities to bridge the gap between the verbal and mathematical realms by composing stories or narratives based on mathematical patterns or relationships. Then teams will exchange narratives with one another, deciphering the patterns or relationships that are expressed or embedded within their respective texts, retranslating them into mathematical form. Through this process, they develop algebraic thinking skills and learn to analyze the structure of a pattern and how it grows or changes.

> ### Skills/State Standards
> ✗ Patterns and relationships
> ✗ Algebraic thinking

Materials You Need

- *Mathematales* reproducible (page 139)
- Sample pattern stories for modeling the activity
- Overhead projector and supplies

Getting Ready

Plan to give each team a different number pattern or have all teams use the same pattern as the basis for their stories. Make student handouts using the *Mathematales* reproducible.

Having a few sample stories will help with the modeling portion of the activity. To stimulate variety and creativity among the teams, model the activity using a different pattern than the one students will use. Some picture books based on mathematical relationships may also serve as good illustrations.

Introducing the Activity

Review different number patterns, such as Kaprekar's sequence, Pascal's triangle, the 100 square, or the Fibonacci sequence, as well as other general number patterns (repeated addition or multiplication of a number, doubling or halving a number, missing numbers in a sequence, etc.).

Have students listen for any patterns in this story:

> There once was a monkey named Goby who liked to swing from branch to branch, picking bananas. Every time Goby would swing to a tree, he would pick double the number of bananas he picked before. After swinging all afternoon, Goby had too many bananas to hold and had to find a place to store them.

After students identify the pattern within the story, discuss how this simple pattern of equations applies: $1 \times 2 = 2$; $2 \times 2 = 4$; $2 \times 6 = 12$; etc. Explain that to "do math" (and algebra) often means to look for and understand patterns. These patterns can come in many shapes and sizes, but they all have one thing in common—something within the pattern that is repeated, extended, or built upon in some way.

Tell students that in this activity, they will use a mathematical pattern as the basis for a story like the one about Goby. Then, they will exchange completed stories and try to figure out the mathematical patterns within each other's narratives.

Modeling the Activity

1. Using an overhead transparency, show students one or more sample mathematical patterns. Brainstorm with them how these patterns could be incorporated into a story.

2. Show students a sample story (or picture book) based on one of the patterns discussed. Have them figure out which of the sample patterns is embedded within the story.

3. Explain that word problems are often like short stories, expressing in words an inherent mathematical relationship or pattern. To encourage creativity, remind students that when writing a story, they should make it fun and challenging to decipher the pattern within the text. If necessary, review the basic elements of stories with students.

Activity in Practice

1. Divide the class into small teams and distribute copies of the *Mathematales* handout. Give each team a mathematical pattern to use as the basis for a story.

2. Have students first discuss the pattern with their team, then complete Part 1 of the handout individually. Ask students to collaborate with team members to complete Part 2.

3. Allow time for teams to draft and revise their stories. Then, collect the final drafts and redistribute them randomly among the teams to "solve" the patterns. After students have read at least one other story, have them pitch their hypothesis about the pattern to the class, verifying their findings with the authoring team.

4. Another possibility is to publish the stories in a class notebook, including blank pages after each story. Then, as teams work together to figure out the pattern, they can use the blank pages to record their work.

5. If time allows, have students make generalizations or predictions about each pattern, discussing how it changes depending on the different numbers, arrangements, or operations involved.

Extension

Use this activity as a warm-up before students examine and write their own word problems.

Pattern Puzzles

Description

In this activity, students practice identifying patterns and relationships and use algebraic thinking to determine the parts of a mathematical problem. As a class, students are given cards containing the parts of a pattern or the steps in a problem. Students must then share their pieces of these mathematical puzzles and fit them together to determine the patterns or solve the problems.

Skills/State Standards

✗ Patterns and relationships
✗ Algebraic thinking

Materials You Need

- Sample patterns and problems for modeling the activity
- Cards containing steps to a problem and/or parts of a pattern (cards could be color-coded, cut like puzzle pieces, or uniform in shape/color)
- Overhead transparency and supplies

Getting Ready

Prepare problem cards that contain parts of a pattern or the steps in a problem. If students initially need more guidance with this activity, consider creating the problem cards as puzzle-like pieces that fit together. Another idea is to color code the cards to facilitate quicker solutions. Then, have students practice the activity again with cards that are uniform in shape and color. Decide beforehand whether the solutions or keys will be included on cards or if, after fitting together the parts, students will then solve the math puzzles.

Introducing the Activity

Have students fill in the missing letter in this pattern: A, __, C. Explain that the alphabet is an example of a pattern or sequence, just like a series of numbers. Ask students how they would solve this problem: A = 1, B = 2, so what is A + B? Explain that patterns and problems include necessary parts; each part can be used as a clue to help identify the pattern or solve the problem. Remind students that knowing how to recognize patterns and the steps in a problem is a skill they will need both in everyday life and on the standardized tests they will take.

Tell students that in this activity, they will use the mathematical fragments on cards they've been given to identify problems and patterns. They will work together, first as a class and then in small teams, to figure out how each set of cards fits together like a puzzle to form a whole pattern or solve a problem.

Modeling the Activity

1. Start with two or three simple problems, then divide them into their major parts or steps. The patterns/problems could involve, for example, a series of shapes based on decreasing or increasing area or a sequence of numbers determined by a specific operation.

2. Using an overhead transparency, draw a grid and write each part randomly in each section of the grid.

3. Show the transparency to students and have them work with you to piece together the different parts for each pattern.

4. Next, using the same transparency grid format, present a word problem to students that has been broken down into separate sentence parts or steps. Guide students as they put the sentence parts into the correct sequence. Then, ask them to try to solve the problem.

5. Present another problem involving several steps and including the solution. Explain that students can use the backwards strategy to help solve some types of problems—working from the solution back through the steps, doing the problem in reverse.

Activity in Practice

1. Distribute the math puzzle cards containing problem steps or pattern parts, giving each student at least one card. The number of cards will depend on the number of students and the steps/parts involved in each problem.

2. Instruct students to circulate around the room, share the parts on their math puzzle cards, and eventually find others with the parts for the same problems. Explain that they must then work together to figure out which math puzzle cards work together to form a complete problem/pattern and possibly find its solution. Once students have formed their teams, have each team use a sheet of paper to identify and record the steps/parts for each problem/pattern.

3. After all of the teams have finished the activity, have the students share their experiences as a class. Ask students to talk about the ways they "solved" the math puzzles and discuss how these skills are transferable to what they might see on the standardized test.

Extensions

For more advanced practice, consider having students develop their own math puzzles for classmates to solve.

For a variation, have each student team create a shape, expression, or other mathematical pattern. The students in each team would then draw a card from a stack that contains a process or situation, apply the process to their creation, and determine how their pattern would change.

Geo Road Trip

Description

In this activity, students will apply geometry and measurements as they plan and map out local road trips. Using where they live as their point of departure, they will plan their trips, looking for and incorporating different aspects of geometry and measurement. Later, they will plot points as coordinates on a grid and determine distances and geometric shapes based on their itineraries.

> ### Skills/State Standards
> ✗ Geometry and spatial reasoning
> ✗ Measurement

Materials You Need

- *Geo Road Trip* reproducibles (page 140 and 141)
- Sample trip for modeling activity
- Local city and state maps
- Measurement tools (rulers, protractors, grid/tracing paper)
- Overhead projector and supplies

Getting Ready

Collect a quantity of state or local road maps, one per team.
You may wish to review map-reading skills with students before working on this activity. Make a transparency copy and student handouts using the *Geo Road Trip* reproducible on page 140. Also make transparency copies of the grid on page 141 to use during the modeling portion of the activity and for students to use when creating coordinate graphs.

Introducing the Activity

Ask students what the prefix *geo-* might mean, considering the words *geography* and *geometry*. Explain that *geo-* means "earth." *Geometry* is literally "measurement of the earth," and *geography* means "description of the earth."

Show students part of your city or town map and ask them what the best route would be to get from point A to point B and then to point C. Remind students of the mathematical phrase: "The shortest distance between two points is a straight line." Over the map, show students how those points connect via straight lines rather than through streets. Explain that when trying to get from one place to another, we need to follow paths, streets, or highways. These routes can form different geometric shapes and lines, like points on a grid. If we traveled only in straight lines, we would be able to see the geometry of our travels.

Tell students that in this activity, they will plan a road trip from their street, town, or city to nearby or faraway places in their state. As they plan their trips, they will look for and include different geometric lines, patterns, and measurements.

Modeling the Activity

1. Using an overhead transparency, show students a state map that includes your city or town. Discuss where you might want to go if you were to cycle or drive within a specific mile radius.

2. Using a transparency pen, plot your potential trip by drawing straight lines between each destination point on the map. Lead students to identify any parallel, congruent, and perpendicular lines or geometrical shapes contained in your route.

3. Next, place the transparency of a grid over your map. Ask students to help you plot the points of your trip. Using a different colored transparency pen, give each point a coordinate on the grid and write the ordered pair as whole numbers.

4. Choose a particular geometrical shape and ask students to help you figure out where you would travel to create that shape on the map and grid, either starting from your town/city or from another point on the map.

5. Create a dilation, translation (slide), or rotation of that shape, and have students help you figure out the major locations for those new sets of coordinates.

6. You could also ask students different questions, such as "If I were to drive through City A, City B, City C, and City D, what shape would my route form?" or "What cities form a triangle (circle or parallelogram) at the following coordinates?"

7. Show students how to measure the length of the trip by figuring out the total distance in miles or meters.

Activity in Practice

1. Divide the class into teams of two students. Distribute copies of the *Geo Road Trip* handout, the transparency of a grid, and copies of area maps to each team.

2. Once the handouts are complete, have each team make a transparency of the planned trip on the map and record the coordinates on the transparency of the overlaying grid.

3. Have each pair share its trip's itinerary with the class. Then, post the *Geo Road Trips* in a public place for other students to view.

Extension

Consider giving students maps of different areas of the country and having them develop geographic scavenger hunts for other teams using their maps.

Amusement Architects

Description

In this activity, students will use different geometric shapes to create and build three-dimensional scale models of original theme parks. As they plan the major features of their parks, students will use polyhedrons as the underlying shapes for each building and attraction. Then, they will determine different measurements (volume, area, and perimeter) of the shapes used and create a scale to represent the differences in size between the models and actual theme parks.

> ### *Skills/State Standards*
> X Geometry and spatial reasoning
> X Measurement

Materials You Need

- *Amusement Architects* reproducible (page 142)
- Sample city maps, theme park maps, and tourist attraction brochures
- Plastic or wooden models of various polyhedrons
- Supplies to make shapes (paper/poster board, rulers, scissors, tape/glue)
- Overhead projector and supplies

Getting Ready

Have examples of each solid shape to be used for the activity available for students.

Make student handouts using the *Amusement Architects* reproducible.

Introducing the Activity

Ask students to think about any theme or amusement parks they have visited. What were their favorite rides? How was the theme carried throughout all aspects of the park?

Then, ask students to think about the major buildings in those parks or in your local town or city. What types of three-dimensional solids serve as the basis for those buildings? Which ones look like rectangular or triangular prisms, spheres, or cylinders? Maybe some buildings are a combination of solids, like the city hall or capitol—a rectangular prism topped with a cylinder and a sphere.

Explain that most of the solid shapes they see are based on two-dimensional plane figures—flat shapes like squares, triangles, circles, and rectangles. Tell students that in this activity, they will get a chance to be their own amusement park architects, working in teams to design their own theme parks. After they design their theme park in a two-dimensional drawing, each team will build a scale model using three-dimensional solids based on plane figures to determine its geometric measurements.

Modeling the Activity

1. Show students some sample amusement park maps that include drawings of key architectural buildings and other attractions. Ask them to brainstorm the major types of buildings and features of a theme park. Use an overhead transparency to create a list.

2. Discuss what types of shapes and solids could be the basis for different types of buildings and rides. Talk about plane figures and their representation into solid form as well as polyhedrons based on polygons.

3. On a blank transparency, sketch your own sample version of a theme park plan, using some of the features from the brainstormed list. Demonstrate how a simple polygon or plane figure can represent each building shape.

4. Working with a sample three-dimensional shape, show students how the plane figure drawings on your map translate into solid forms for one of your theme park's buildings or rides.

5. Using that example, show students how to determine the model size and actual size of the figure and then determine its volume, area, and/or perimeter.

Activity in Practice

1. Divide the class into architectural firms and distribute copies of the *Amusement Architects* handout. Decide upon the shapes and solids to include in their theme parks and have students make notes on the handout.

2. As students work on their designs, have them look at other examples of amusement park maps for inspiration and ideas.

3. Once teams are finished with their designs and have completed the handout, have them build scale models of their theme parks. They could use paper-constructed shapes or found objects for the shapes in the model.

4. Have students determine the appropriate measurements for the shapes in their models and also figure out what the scale for each theme park would be if it were actually constructed.

5. After each firm has completed its scale model, have a viewing day and invite students from other classes to tour the theme parks and vote on their favorites.

Extension

This activity could be adapted to different scenarios: design a new town hall, a new school, or even a new city.

You Rule!

Description

In this activity, students will apply measurement concepts to devise their own systems of measurement. They will use these systems to measure various objects, then compare their systems to other units of measurement. They will also use their systems to help solve mathematical problems that require measurement as a part of the problem-solving process.

Skills/State Standards

X Measurement

X Mathematical processes and problem solving

Materials You Need

- *You Rule!* reproducible (page 143)
- Sample measurement system and tool for modeling activity
- Measuring tools: ruler, yardstick, meterstick, clock, thermometer, scale, measuring cup, calendar
- Overhead projector and supplies

Getting Ready

This activity will work well as a review for different forms of measurement.

Make student handouts using the *You Rule!* reproducible. Also make an additional copy on a transparency to use during the modeling portion of the activity.

Introducing the Activity

Ask students to guesstimate the height of the Statue of Liberty or some local landmark of notable size. If they give their guesses in feet, ask them why they chose that unit of measurement instead of another one—why not inches, or meters, or miles? Explain how the type of measurement we use depends on the situation—both its context and its size.

Explain that we use units of measurement not only to figure out the length, size, or distance of something but also to help us solve problems. Tell students that in this activity, they will apply what they know about measurement units and devise their own system of measurement. They will then apply this system in different contexts, using it to determine size and/or distance as well as to help solve problems.

Modeling the Activity

1. Show students samples of different measuring tools (ruler, yardstick, meterstick, clock, thermometer, scale, measuring cup, calendar) and discuss how these tools are utilized by particular systems of measurement.

2. Place the transparency on the overhead projector and use the measurement system chart to discuss with students how different systems compare. Explain the difference between the metric and customary systems of measurement as well as how the use of different types of systems depends on what is being measured.

3. Use the transparency as the basis for a sample measurement system to model for students.

4. For each step, explain how you applied what you already knew about measurement to create your own unique system.

5. For Step 4 on the handout, use a premade tool to show and demonstrate its use before completing Step 5.

6. Select one or two measurement problems and work through them with the students, applying the sample system.

Activity in Practice

1. Divide the class into teams of two students and distribute copies of the *You Rule!* handout to each student. Decide whether to allow students to base their systems on any of the major three systems measurement (time, length, mass/weight) or have them focus on one particular system.

2. Have each pair work on the handout together, brainstorming on one handout and using the other to record their final ideas and responses.

3. Show students the supplies that are available before they begin to design their measuring tools. You may need to limit what the tools can be made of according to available resources.

4. Decide beforehand what problems the students will solve for Step 5 on the handout and distribute them to each pair.

5. After each team has completed the handout, consider one of the following team activities:

   a. *Measuring Match*—Two sets of student pairs read a problem to solve, each using their own measurement system. They must then explain their solutions and let the class decide which pair wins a point for that round.

   b. *Measurement Riddles*—Each student pair writes several riddles that use their own measurement system. Other students are challenged to apply another particular system to solve each riddle. For example: "How many *zippees* is it from San Diego to New York City?"

Extensions

Students could also determine the perimeter and area of objects based on their own measurement system. As a crossover activity, students could write original stories about their measurement system and its "history."

Wacky Stats

Description

In this activity, students will collect statistical information about the personal habits of their classmates—such as food consumption, retail purchases, personal favorites—and use that data to determine a total measurement of mass, length, or volume. They will then transform that total into a three-dimensional representation (sculpture, graph, or other form of display) revealing the scale and scope of that measurement.

Skills/State Standards
X Probability and statistics
X Graphing

Materials You Need
- Copies of the *Wacky Stats* reproducible (page 144)
- Overhead projector and supplies

Getting Ready

This activity can be organized as a class project or by working in collaborative teams. Make student handouts using the *Wacky Stats* reproducible.

Introducing the Activity

Ask students to guess how many cartons of orange juice are consumed in the United States each year. What about soda, cookies, pizza, or ice cream? Explain that these numbers are examples of statistics or an organized collection of numerical facts. Tell students that statistics are collected to help answer questions and solve problems. They are often displayed graphically to illustrate their impact and help people to interpret and understand them.

Tell students that in this activity they will wear the wacky hats of statisticians, collecting unusual facts and representing them in a very fun, visual way. During this process, they will be creative in both the collection and representation of their statistics.

Modeling the Activity

1. Using an overhead transparency or chalkboard, ask students to brainstorm the types of numerical facts they might be able to collect at school, at home, or in their community. For example, what is the most popular type of running shoe or how many students say their favorite color is green? How many cartons of chocolate milk are consumed during one week, month, or year at their school?

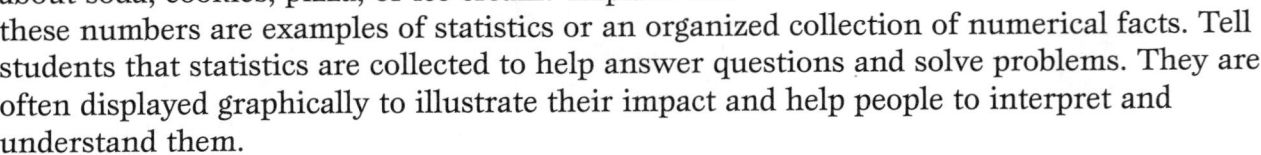

2. Explain that the reason people gather facts is to help answer a question or solve a problem in some way. Make comparisons between this mathematical process and the steps involved in the scientific process: thinking of a problem or question, developing a hypothesis, collecting data, reflecting, and drawing a conclusion.

3. After thinking of several different types of statistics to gather, share with students a statistic related to a question, such as "What is the highest grossing (or most popular) movie of all time?" Discuss how someone might collect information about that question to answer it. Would they stand outside of theaters and ask people what they were going to see? Or would they base their answer on ticket sales?

4. Have students work with you to think of other related statistics you could gather—for example, the most popular movie genres. Ask students how you might display those numerical facts in a graph.

5. Show students a sample graph such as pie, bar, or histograph that displays the statistics.

6. Next, ask students how you could get really graphic with your data—what type of three-dimensional display would make an impact, both visually and mentally? Brainstorm some possibilities together. For example, if they tabulated the total number of cartons of chocolate milk consumed in one month, they might make a giant chocolate milk carton representing the total volume of milk consumed.

7. Ask students what someone could learn from thinking about the results of the numerical facts gathered. Explain that thinking about the results is part of the process of interpreting and analyzing the information.

Activity in Practice

1. Have students form wacky stats teams. Decide whether the class will work together on aspects of the same question or problem or if each team will base its data collection on a unique question or problem.

2. Distribute copies of the *Wacky Stats* handout to each team.

3. Once the handouts are complete, direct the students to collect their data and represent it on a graph. Then, have each team select an idea from Step 4 for the three-dimensional display. Encourage the students to gather the necessary materials and make the large three-dimensional representation of the statistic(s) collected.

4. Display and advertise the class's projects. Invite parents to view the completed projects.

Extension

This activity can be altered to fit specifically with curriculum content. Students could gather information concerning assigned content-related issues, pull out essential facts, determine their numerical significance, and represent those numbers graphically on a small scale (two-dimensional drawing of a graph, etc.) or a large scale (a three-dimensional representation).

No Problem

Description

In this activity, students will identify a problem in their school or community and apply problem-solving strategies to develop a solution that involves mathematical reasoning and skills. As they develop a problem-solving process, they draw upon related mathematical concepts and skills, using them in a real-world context. In this format, students will solve problems that arise in different contexts, apply and adapt a variety of appropriate strategies to solve these problems, and monitor and reflect on the process of mathematical problem solving they used.

> ### Skills/State Standards
>
> X Mathematical processes and problem solving

Materials You Need

- *No Problem* reproducible (page 145)
- Sample problems for modeling activity
- Overhead projector and supplies

Getting Ready

Consider reviewing different problem-solving techniques with the class in terms of another discipline, such as a science experiment. Have newspapers or newsletters on hand for sample problems and for brainstorming.

Make student handouts using the *No Problem* reproducible.

Introducing the Activity

Ask students to define the word *problem*. After students share their definitions, discuss with them how the word can be used for a variety of situations and issues. Ask students to brainstorm issues or problems in their local community (school or city). Maybe the school does not have a recycling program, or maybe there aren't enough bicycle paths in the city for people to use. Discuss how math can be used to help solve problems on different levels, not just the problems in a textbook.

Tell students that they will work in teams to identify a local problem and develop a solution that uses mathematical reasoning and skills. They will use these skills to incorporate math in their steps to solve the problem.

Modeling the Activity

1. Choose an example of a problem or issue in the school or local community that involves mathematical operations and reasoning in some way. For example, if the school does not serve macaroni and cheese, how could they go about adding it to the menu? Or, if the school does not currently recycle, what would it take to start a recycling program? Or, how could the school support the local homeless shelter or food bank?

2. Show students the problem-solving process that can be adapted to address such a problem. Review the major steps for solving a mathematical problem and add any applicable details such as:

   - Define and understand the problem.
   - Gather and process information.
   - Design a plan.
   - Carry out the plan.
   - Evaluate the plan.
   - Share the solution.

3. Using the sample issue or problem, discuss how each step of the problem-solving process would be applied.

4. Review some of the problem-solving strategies that students use in mathematics that would apply to solving this type of problem: drawing a picture, looking for a pattern, systematic guessing and checking, acting it out, making a table, working a simpler problem, or working backwards to solve a problem.

5. Explain that when they are working in teams, they may need to assign responsibility for each part of the process.

Activity in Practice

1. Divide the class into small teams and distribute copies of the *No Problem* handout. Have teams select issues or problems that involve math in some way. If possible, supply a working list of ideas and brainstorm other possibilities before teams begin the activity.

2. When the teams have completed Steps 1 through 3 as outlined on the handout, have them implement their plans and record their results.

3. After every team has implemented a plan, have students evaluate the results, including the math involved in reaching a solution.

4. Ask the students to present their plan and solutions to the rest of the class, then discuss how math played a part in the problem-solving process.

Extension

If students have difficulty coming up with an issue or problem, assign teams a specific topic with its mathematical aspects briefly outlined for them.

Time Flies

Step 1. Think about how you spend your time during one day. Using the chart below, estimate how much time you spend every day doing each of the listed activities.

General Activity	Estimated Time (Hours)	Estimated Percentage
Being in school		
Sleeping		
Eating		
Playing/recreation		
Doing homework		
Doing chores		
Enjoying hobbies		
Other:		

Step 2. Using the chart on the *Weekly Log* handout, keep track of how you actually spend your time each day. In the space provided, list your activities for each time segment.

Step 3. Using your weekly log as a reference, divide your activities into the major categories shown in the chart below. Then, figure out the total amount of time (in hours/minutes) devoted to each category. Calculate the times for each category as fractional and percentage amounts.

General Activity	Total Time (Hours/Minutes)	Fractional Amount	Percentage Amount
Being in school			
Sleeping			
Eating			
Playing/recreation			
Doing homework			
Doing chores			
Enjoying hobbies			
Other:			

Step 4. On a separate sheet of paper, create a pie chart showing each category and the percentage amounts based on the information recorded in Step 3.

Weekly Log

Time	Mon.	Tues.	Wed.	Thurs.	Fri.	Sat.	Sun.
6:00 A.M.							
6:30 A.M.							
7:00 A.M.							
7:30 A.M.							
8:00 A.M.							
8:30 A.M.							
9:00 A.M.							
9:30 A.M.							
10:00 A.M.							
10:30 A.M.							
11:00 A.M.							
11:30 A.M.							
12:00 P.M.							
12:30 P.M.							
1:00 P.M.							
1:30 P.M.							
2:00 P.M.							
2:30 P.M.							
3:00 P.M.							
3:30 P.M.							
4:00 P.M.							
4:30 P.M.							
5:00 P.M.							
5:30 P.M.							
6:00 P.M.							
6:30 P.M.							
7:00 P.M.							
7:30 P.M.							
8:00 P.M.							
8:30 P.M.							
9:00 P.M.							
9:30 P.M.							
10:00 P.M. – 6:00 A.M. (8 hours)							

Marketplace Mayhem

Step 1. Product

Product name: _____

Product's Main Materials/Ingredients	Cost of Each Material/Product	Amount Needed to Make One Product

Step 2. Target Audience

What types of people, businesses, or organizations will most likely buy your product? _____

_____

Where will you place your product for sale? _____

_____

Step 3. Costs and Estimated Profits

Do research about your product and use that information to complete these questions. Use a separate sheet of paper to show your work.

What will it cost to make one product item (from ingredients or materials to packaging)?	
What equipment, machinery, or supplies will you need? How much will they cost?	
What type of workforce will you need (if you need one)? How much will you pay employees?	
How many products will you make per month? Per year?	
What should be the selling price of the product?	
How many do you need to sell to make a profit in one month or one year?	
What, if any, are the advertising costs?	

Classified Careers

Step 1. Choosing a Job

Read through the classifieds for a job you would like to have, then write it in the chart below. Use the income information to fill in the other boxes in the chart.

Job Title	
Weekly Income	
Monthly Income	
Annual Income	

Step 2. Making a Budget

Using the categories below, fill in the chart with the amount you can afford for each month on the basis of your monthly income. Use information from the newspaper to figure out the costs for some of the categories, such as rent, transportation, and entertainment.

Budget Category	Monthly Amount	Fractional Amount	Percentage Amount
Rent/Housing			
Car/Transportation			
Food			
Entertainment			
Utilities			
Savings			
Purchases			
Other:			

Step 3. Making a Budget Chart or Graph

Use a separate sheet of paper to make a pie chart or bar graph showing your budget categories and their percentage amounts.

Step 4. Figuring Costs

Look through all sections of the newspaper and choose at least three items you would like to purchase. Write those items and their costs on the lines below.

Item 1: _____   Cost: _____
Item 2: _____   Cost: _____
Item 3: _____   Cost: _____

Can you afford these items or not? Explain your answer on the back of this sheet. Use basic math to support your answer.

Money Madness

Place Value Mat

Billions Period			Millions Period			Thousands Period			Ones Period			Decimal	Tenths	Hundredths
Hundreds	Tens	Ones	Hundreds	Tens	Ones	Hundreds	Tens	Ones	Hundreds	Tens	Ones			
												.		

Directions: For each question, use the space below to figure out an answer and show your work.

Starting Amount of Money:

$ ____ ____ ____ ____ ____ ____ ____ ____ ____ ____ . ____ ____

1.

2.

3.

4.

5.

Mathematales

Part 1.

Write the number pattern your team will use for the story below.

Write three ideas you have for a story that uses your team's pattern.

1. _____
2. _____
3. _____

Use the chart below to map out one of your ideas for a story.

Setting	
Characters	
Major Events/ Problems in Story	
Solution/ Ending of Story	

Part 2.

Share your story ideas with your teammates. Then, work together to write a rough draft of your story on the back of this sheet or on a separate sheet of paper.

Geo Road Trip

Directions: Work with your partner to plan your road trip by completing each step of this sheet.

1. Look at the map and select the locations you plan to visit. Then mark those locations on the map.

   Make sure to include the following geometric elements in your itinerary:
   - Parallel, perpendicular, and congruent lines
   - A geometric shape such as a parallelogram, triangle, rectangle, or another polygon

   Write the names of the places you will visit on your road trip in order from beginning to end:

   _____

   _____

   _____

   What shape will the path of your road trip make?_____

   _____

2. Place a transparency (or tracing paper) grid over the map. Number the axes of your grid. Label each destination on your trip as a coordinate, with an ordered pair of whole numbers.

3. Create a translation, rotation, or reflection of your trip's geometric shape and label those points on your map's coordinate grid. Use ordered pairs of whole numbers.

4. Measure the total distance of your trip and figure out its length using the units of measurement listed below:

   Miles: _____

   Kilometers:_____

   Meters: _____

   Feet: _____

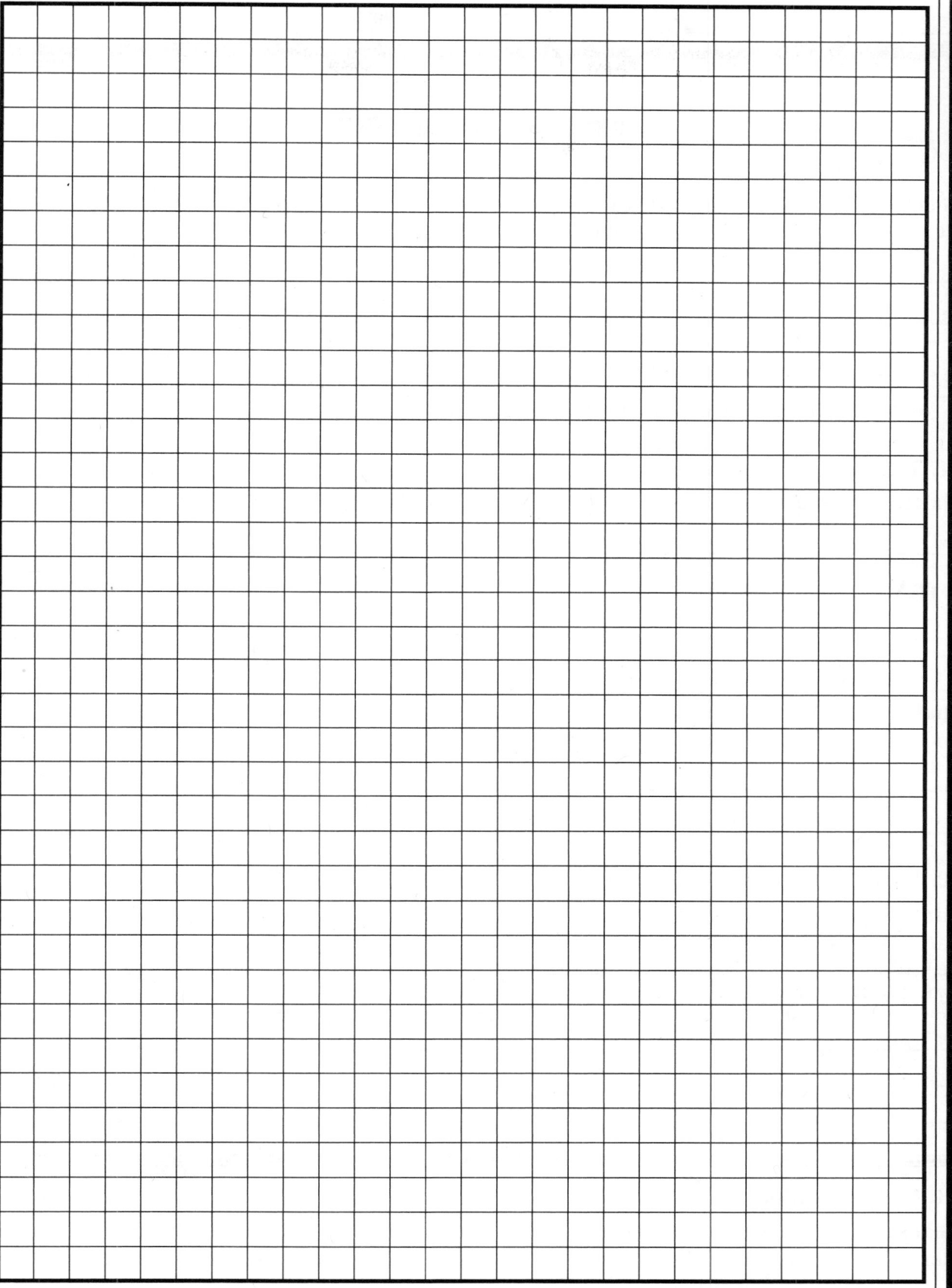

CD-2238 *Teamwork Test Prep*

Amusement Architects

Directions: Working with your architectural team, design and make a model of a theme park that includes a total of _____ plane figures, solids, and polyhedrons from the following list:

_____   _____   _____   _____

_____   _____   _____   _____

The total perimeter of your theme park will be _____.

The total area of your theme park will be _____.

Step 1. Thinking of Theme

What are some possible themes for your theme park? List your ideas below.

_____

Given the theme, what are some rides and attractions that should be in your theme park?

_____

_____

What are some other important things to include in your theme park? (For example: concession stands, restrooms, walkways, storage areas, parking, etc.)

_____

_____

Step 2. Using Shapes and Solids

Think about the shape of each ride, attraction, or building in your theme park. Fill in the chart below with your ideas. Use the back of this page if you need more space.

Theme Park Building/Ride/Attraction	Basic Shape

Step 3. Making a Model

Use a separate sheet of paper to make a basic two-dimensional sketch of your theme park. Then, use your sketch to make a scale model of your theme park, using solid shapes for each building, ride, or other feature.

You Rule!

Step 1. Give your measurement system an original name: _____

Step 2. What would someone use your system to take measurements for? Write some ideas on the lines below.

_____   _____   _____

_____   _____   _____

_____   _____   _____

Step 3. Compare your measurement system with one of the systems in the chart below. Then, use the space under the chart to record your comparisons.
Example: 1 zippee = 4 inches

Step 4. What would a measurement tool based on your system look like? Sketch your measurement tool on a sheet of paper. Then make the tool and use it for step 5.

Units of Linear Measurement	Units of Time Measurement	Mass and Weight
1 kilometer = 1,000 meters	1 year = 365 days	1 kilogram = 1,000 grams
1 meter = 100 centimeters	1 year = 12 months	1 gram = 1,000 milligrams
1 centimeter = 10 millimeters	1 year = 52 weeks	1 ton = 2,000 pounds
1 mile = 1,760 yards	1 week = 7 days	1 pound = 16 ounces
1 mile = 5,280 feet	1 day = 24 hours	
1 yard = 3 feet	1 hour = 60 minutes	
1 foot = 12 inches	1 minute = 60 seconds	

Step 5. Use your new measurement tool to measure the following items. Record your answers in the spaces provided.

Item to Measure	Total Measurement (in your system's units)

Solve the problems from your teacher using your measurement system. Use the back of this sheet or a separate sheet of paper to show your work.

Wacky Stats

1. WHAT numerical fact(s) will your team collect information about?

   _____

   _____

   _____

2. WHERE or from WHOM will you collect information about the numerical fact(s)?

   _____

   _____

   HOW will you collect and organize the information?

   _____

   _____

3. HOW will you display your wacky stats? What type of chart or graph will you use?

   _____

   _____

4. Write down your ideas for a three-dimensional display of your statistics that would make an impact, both visually and mentally.

   _____

   _____

   _____

   _____

No Problem

Directions: Choose a problem from your local community and use the following problem-solving process to reach a solution. Use the space provided or a separate sheet to record your work for each step of the process.

1. Explain Your Problem
   - *What are you asked to find/solve?*
   - *What words do you need to know?*
   - *What type of math might be involved?*

2. Collect Information
   - *What other information do you need?*

3. Design a Plan
   - *Which strategies will your team use to reach a solution?*
     (Examples: Drawing a picture, looking for a pattern, guessing systematically, acting it out, making a table)
   - *What steps are involved?*
   - *What types of math will you use in your plan?*

4. Apply Your Plan
   - *How will you carry out your plan?*
   - *What are the outcomes of your plan?*

5. Think about Your Plan
   - *How effective was your solution?*
   - *Is the problem solved?*

6. Share the Solution
   - *How will you share your solution?*

Practice Math Test—Grade 5

Name: _____

Date: _____ Class: _____

Directions: This test contains 30 math problems, a math reference chart, and an answer sheet. Read each problem carefully. Mark your answers on your answer sheet. If you do not understand a question, ask your teacher for help.

Note to Teacher: This chapter contains a reproducible practice test based on the most common math standards tested nationwide at the fifth-grade level. This practice test can be given to your students before, during, or after they have completed the activities in Chapter 7. (For a short diagnostic test, see Chapter 3.)

Practice Math Test—Grade 5 (continued)

How to Use Your Answer Sheet

Read each question and choose the best answer. Mark each answer on your answer sheet by filling in the correct bubble.

Sample 1   The school bus was $\frac{2}{3}$ empty.

What percent of the bus was empty?

A   40%

B   75%

C   25%

D   60%   **Answer:**   Ⓐ Ⓑ Ⓒ ⬤D

For some questions, you will be asked to determine the answer and fill in a grid on your answer sheet. There may be more than one correct way to fill in the grid. Follow these steps:

1. Work the problem and find an answer.
2. Write your answer in the boxes across the top of the grid.
    - Print only one digit or symbol in each box.
    - Be sure to write a dollar sign, fraction bar, or decimal point in the answer box if it is part of the answer.
3. Fill in the corresponding bubble in each column.
    Do NOT fill in bubbles in the empty columns.

Sample 2   Mario bought a CD for $13.25, including tax. He paid for the CD with a $20 bill. How much change did Mario receive?

Answer: $6.75

Math Reference Chart — 1

	Customary	**Metric**
Length	1 foot = 12 inches 1 yard = 3 feet 1 mile = 1,760 yards 1 mile = 5,280 feet	1 centimeter = 10 millimeters 1 meter = 100 centimeters 1 kilometer = 1,000 meters

	Customary	**Metric**
Mass and Weight	1 pound = 16 ounces 1 ton = 2,000 pounds	1 gram = 1,000 milligrams 1 kilogram = 1,000 grams

	Customary	**Metric**
Capacity	1 cup = 8 ounces 1 pint = 2 cups 1 quart = 2 pints 1 gallon = 4 quarts	1 centiliter = 10 milliliters 1 deciliter = 10 centiliters 1 liter = 1,000 milliliters

Time	1 minute = 60 seconds 1 hour = 60 minutes 1 day = 24 hours 1 week = 7 days	1 year = 365 days 1 year = 52 weeks 1 year = 12 months

Simple Interest	$I = prt$	I = interest p = principal r = rate t = time

continued on next page

Practice Math Test—Grade 5 (continued)

Math Reference Chart — 2

Key

l = length	P = perimeter	A = area
w = width	SA = surface area	V = volume
s = length of a side	d = diameter	B = area of the base of a solid
b = base	r = radius	
h = height	C = circumference	$\pi \approx 3.14$ or $\frac{22}{7}$

The sum of the interior angles of a polygon is equal to $180(n - 2)$,
where n is the number of sides in the polygon.

Perimeter

square $P = 4s$
rectangle $P = 2(l + w)$

Circumference

circle $C = 2\pi r$ or πd

Pythagorean Theorem

$a^2 + b^2 = c^2$

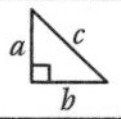

Area

square $A = s^2$
rectangle $A = lw$ or bh
triangle $A = \frac{1}{2}bh$ or $\frac{bh}{2}$
trapezoid $A = \frac{1}{2}(b_1 + b_2)h$ or $\frac{(b_1 + b_2)h}{2}$
parallelogram $A = bh$
circle $A = \pi r^2$

Surface Area

cube $SA = 6s^2$
rectangular solid $SA = 2(lw) + 2(hw) + 2(lh)$
cylinder (total) $SA = 2\pi rh + 2\pi r^2$
sphere $SA = 4\pi r^2$

Volume

rectangular solid $V = lwh$
prism $V = Bh$
cylinder $V = \pi r^2 h$
pyramid $V = \frac{1}{3}Bh$
sphere $V = \frac{4}{3}\pi r^3$

Practice Math Test—Grade 5

1 What are the coordinates of the player closest to the ball?

A (4, 2)

B (5, 6)

C (9, 3)

D (8, 7)

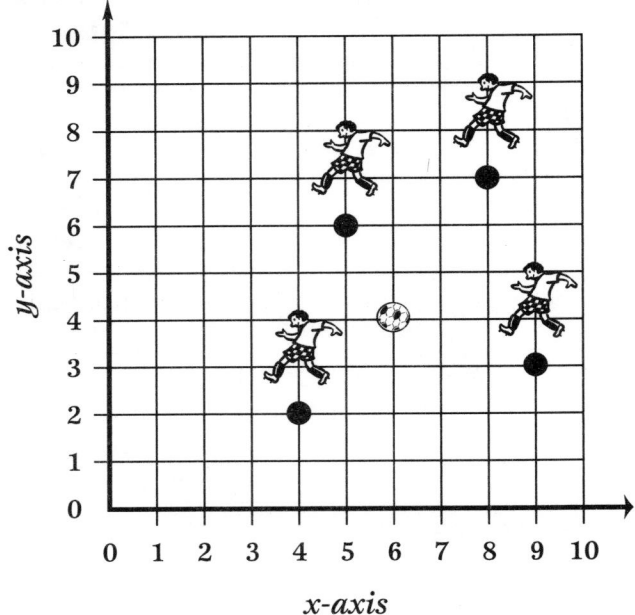

2 Robert and Lisa are using balloons to decorate for a party. They have 34 balloons, and need 12 more to finish. Which operation should be used in the box below to find how many balloons total they will have for the party?

34 ☐ 12

F division

G subtraction

H addition

J multiplication

3 Look at the drawing below.

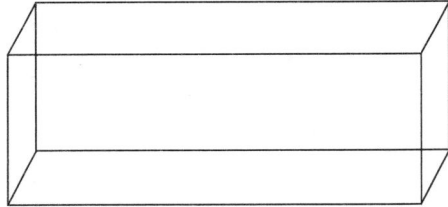

Which statement about this figure is true?

A The figure has no vertices.

B The figure has 2 rectangular faces.

C The figure is a cube.

D The figure has 6 faces.

GO ON

4 Jasmine wants to make some brownies that take 45 minutes to bake. She puts the brownies in the oven at 3:18 P.M. What time will be brownies be done?

F 3:18 P.M.

G 3:45 P.M.

H 4:03 P.M.

J 4:15 P.M.

5 Which number is less than $\frac{2}{3}$?

A $\frac{3}{4}$

B $\frac{4}{5}$

C $\frac{3}{6}$

D $\frac{6}{8}$

6 What does the ____ stand for in the number sentence below?

$$(\underline{\hspace{1cm}} \times 4) + 7 = 43$$

F 7

G 9

H 14

J 32

7 Look at these figures.

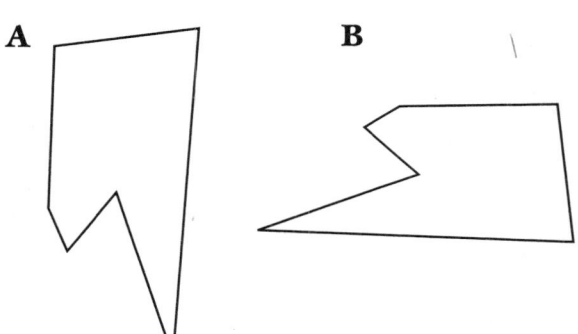

Which of the figures below is NOT similar to the figures above?

A   **B**

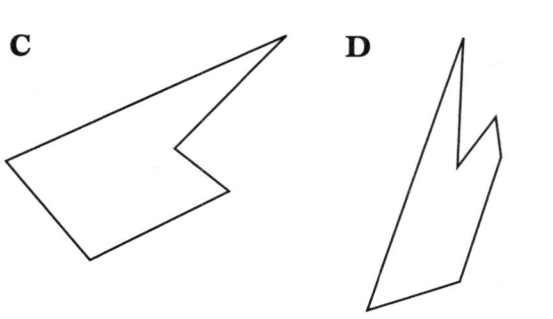

C   **D**

GO ON

8 Kelly has done 3 of 5 math homework problems for school tomorrow. What percent of her homework has Kelly already done?

   F   30%

   G   40%

   H   60%

   J   75%

9 Which units are most likely to be used to measure the length of a soccer field?

   A   millimeters

   B   centimeters

   C   meters

   D   kilometers

10 Veronica wants to find the volume of the figure shown below. The figure is made up of 1" cubes.

What is the volume of this figure?

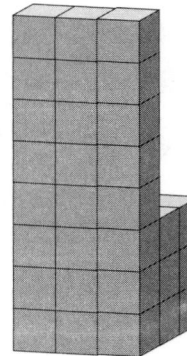

   F   24 in.^{3}

   G   36 in.^{3}

   H   42 in.^{3}

   J   48 in.^{3}

11 In which diagram is the unshaded figure a translation of the shaded figure?

A

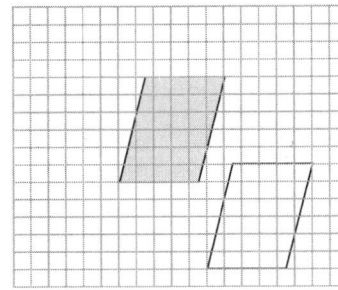

B

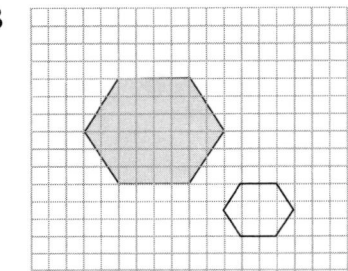

C

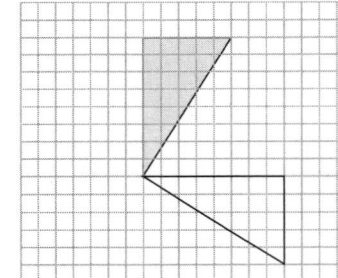

D

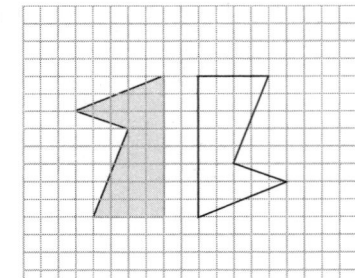

GO ON ➡

Practice Math Test—Grade 5 (continued)

Use the graph below to answer problems 12 and 13.

Greg, Henry, Denise, and Tessa entered the school contest to design a new mascot. The graph below shows the number of votes each student's design received.

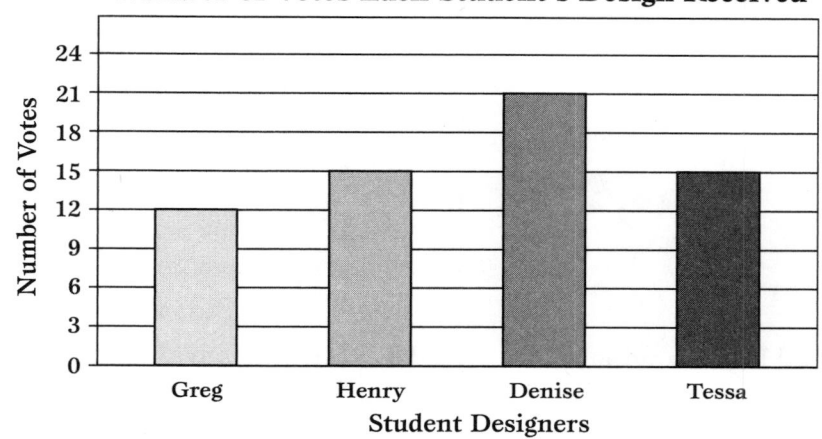

Number of Votes Each Student's Design Received

12 How many more votes did Denise's design receive than Greg's design?

Record your answer below, then fill in the bubbles on your answer sheet. Be sure to use the correct place value.

13 What is the mode of the number of votes from the design contest?

F 12

G 15

H 18

J 21

GO ON

Practice Math Test—Grade 5 (continued)

14 Jamie and Serena each had a box of candy to sell. Jamie sold $\frac{2}{3}$ of his box, and Serena sold more candy than Jamie did. Which fraction of her box of candy could Serena have sold?

A $\frac{1}{2}$

B $\frac{3}{4}$

C $\frac{4}{8}$

D $\frac{3}{5}$

15 A hummingbird can beat its wings about 4,200 times per minute. How many times would a hummingbird beat its wings in one second?

F 60

G 70

H 120

J 400

16 What is 4,356,293 rounded to the nearest hundred thousand?

A 4,300,000

B 4,400,000

C 4,460,000

D 5,300,000

17 A flower shop manager ordered 2 boxes of yellow roses. Each box contained 190 roses. She also ordered 37 carnations and 52 lilies. Which is the best estimate of the total number of roses ordered?

F 300

G 400

H 500

J 520

18 Mr. Jones wants to have a rug made to fit his office floor. The picture below shows the outline of the office floor.

What is the area of the office floor?

A 36 ft.^{2}

B 42 ft.^{2}

C 48 ft.^{2}

D 84 ft.^{2}

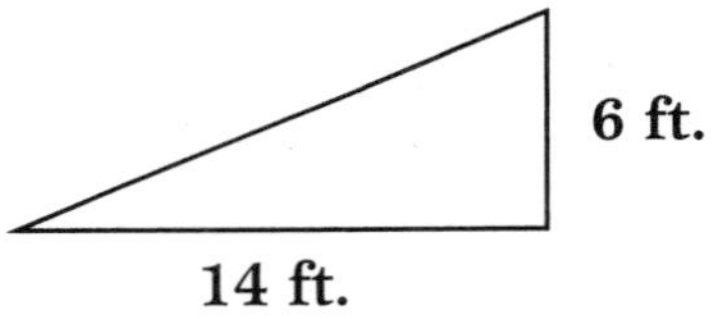

6 ft.

14 ft.

19 Gretchen studied 3 days for a big test. How long, in weeks, did Gretchen study?

F $\frac{2}{7}$

G $\frac{3}{7}$

H $\frac{4}{7}$

J $\frac{5}{7}$

GO ON

Practice Math Test—Grade 5 (continued)

20 The line graph shows 4 points.

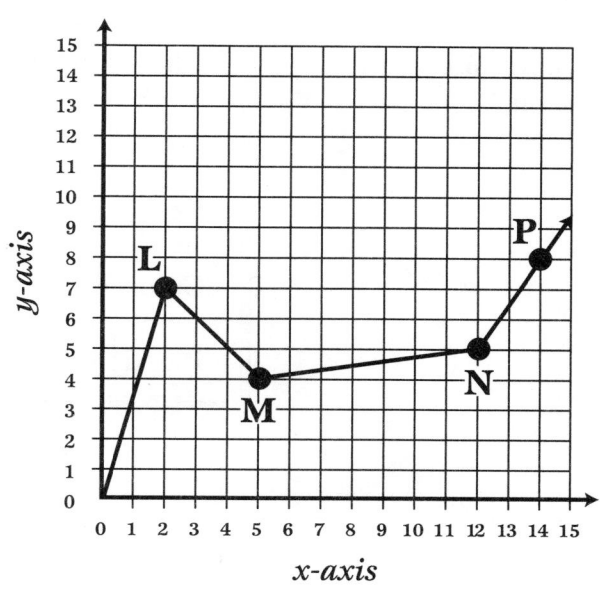

x-axis

Which table shows the coordinates of the points on the line graph above?

A

Point	x	y
L	2	7
M	5	4
N	5	12
P	14	8

B

Point	x	y
L	2	8
M	5	4
N	12	5
P	14	8

C

Point	x	y
L	7	2
M	4	5
N	5	12
P	8	14

D

Point	x	y
L	2	7
M	5	4
N	12	5
P	14	8

GO ON

Practice Math Test—Grade 5 (continued)

21 Olivia is decorating cupcakes for a party. The chart on the right shows the different kinds of decorations she can use. If Olivia decides to use 3 different decorations, how many combinations are possible?

F 15

G 8

H 27

J 10

Cupcake Decorations	
Chocolate sprinkles	
Candy confetti	
Candy flowers	
Colored frosting	FROSTING
Plastic smiley faces	

---

22 Leo is a long-distance bicyclist. The table shows how many miles he can ride in different lengths of time. The numbers form a pattern. What 2 numbers are needed to complete the chart?

Riding Pattern

Number of Hours	1	2	3	4	5	6
Miles Ridden	22	37	52	67		

A 77 and 92

B 82 and 97

C 72 and 92

D 87 and 92

23 The chart below shows the areas of 5 states. Which state has an area that is about one-third the size of California?

State	Area in Square Miles
Colorado	104,100
California	163,707
Kansas	82,282
New York	54,475
Georgia	59,441

F Colorado

G Kansas

H New York

J Georgia

GO ON

Practice Math Test—Grade 5 (continued)

24 Look at the triangle below.

How many triangles of this size would be needed to cover exactly $\frac{1}{2}$ of the shape on the right?

A 5

B 6

C 7

D 9

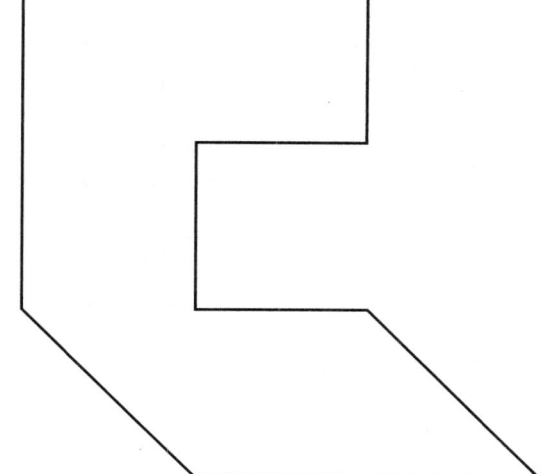

---

25 Sheila and Eric rode their bicycles to the park. Their ride is mapped below.

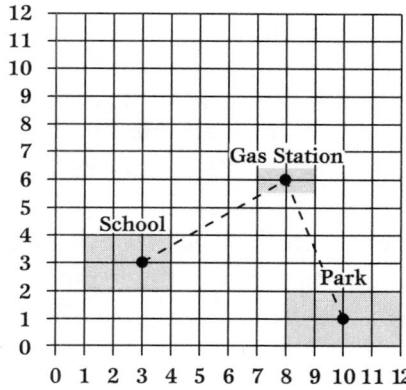

Along the way, they decided to stop at the gas station to fill up their tires. What are the coordinates of the gas station?

F (6, 8)

G (8, 3)

H (8, 6)

J (3, 3)

26 Lak has 3 quarters. He has 4 more dimes than quarters. He has 2 fewer silver dollars than dimes. How much money total does Lak have?

A $3.15

B $3.45

C $5.75

D $6.45

27 What does the digit 3 in the number 35,291 mean?

F 3,000

G 300

H 3,000,000

J 30,000

GO ON ⇒

28 Fifth-grade students kept track of the kinds of fruit they ate with their lunch. They collected the following data.

Fruit Survey

Kind of Fruit	Number of Students
Apple	14
Orange	11
Banana	10
Grapes	8
Pear	7
Total	50

What percentage of the students ate grapes with their lunch?

Record your answer and fill in the bubbles on your answer sheet. Be sure to use the correct place value.

29 Isabel measured an area of a square to be 36 square feet. Aron measured one side of the square to be 6 feet. What is the perimeter of this square?

$$36 \text{ ft.}^2$$

A 12 ft.

B 18 ft.

C 24 ft.

D 36 ft.

30 Colin wants to spend his birthday money at the mall. He has $40.00 to spend. He wants to buy 2 comic books that cost $2.50 each, a shirt for $15.95, and a poster for $8.90. All prices include tax. How much money will be have left after paying for these items?

F $29.85

G $12.65

H $10.15

J $27.35

END OF PRACTICE TEST

Practice Math Test—Grade 5
Answer Sheet

Directions: Mark your answers on this answer sheet. Be sure to fill in each bubble completely and erase any stray marks.

1 Ⓐ Ⓑ Ⓒ Ⓓ

2 Ⓕ Ⓖ Ⓗ Ⓙ

3 Ⓐ Ⓑ Ⓒ Ⓓ

4 Ⓕ Ⓖ Ⓗ Ⓙ

5 Ⓐ Ⓑ Ⓒ Ⓓ

6 Ⓕ Ⓖ Ⓗ Ⓙ

7 Ⓐ Ⓑ Ⓒ Ⓓ

8 Ⓕ Ⓖ Ⓗ Ⓙ

9 Ⓐ Ⓑ Ⓒ Ⓓ

10 Ⓕ Ⓖ Ⓗ Ⓙ

11 Ⓐ Ⓑ Ⓒ Ⓓ

12 [grid-in bubble answer block]

13 Ⓕ Ⓖ Ⓗ Ⓙ

14 Ⓐ Ⓑ Ⓒ Ⓓ

15 Ⓕ Ⓖ Ⓗ Ⓙ

16 Ⓐ Ⓑ Ⓒ Ⓓ

17 Ⓕ Ⓖ Ⓗ Ⓙ

18 Ⓐ Ⓑ Ⓒ Ⓓ

19 Ⓕ Ⓖ Ⓗ Ⓙ

20 Ⓐ Ⓑ Ⓒ Ⓓ

21 Ⓕ Ⓖ Ⓗ Ⓙ

22 Ⓐ Ⓑ Ⓒ Ⓓ

23 Ⓕ Ⓖ Ⓗ Ⓙ

24 Ⓐ Ⓑ Ⓒ Ⓓ

25 Ⓕ Ⓖ Ⓗ Ⓙ

26 Ⓐ Ⓑ Ⓒ Ⓓ

27 Ⓕ Ⓖ Ⓗ Ⓙ

28 [grid-in bubble answer block]

29 Ⓐ Ⓑ Ⓒ Ⓓ

30 Ⓕ Ⓖ Ⓗ Ⓙ

Answer Key

page 20
Diagnostic Reading Test

1	C	2	H
3	B	4	G
5	D	6	F
7	A	8	H
9	B	10	J
11	A	12	G
13	C	14	H
15	C	16	H

page 28
Diagnostic Math Test

1	C	2	H
3	D	4	F
5	B	6	G
7	C	8	J
9	C	10	H
11	B	12	F
13	D	14	H
15	C		

page 94
Practice Reading Test

1	B	2	H
3	D	4	H
5	A	6	G
7	C	8	H
9	C	10	F

11 *Answers will vary.*
Other methods to stop icebergs from hitting the oil platform include spreading carbon black on the bergs, which would absorb sunlight. The icebergs were supposed to melt but turned over instead. Another method was drilling holes with a remote-controlled vehicle. Towlines were to be placed in the holes. The ocean was too rough for this plan to work. Firing a water cannon at the icebergs was also tried. This method only worked on the smaller icebergs.

12	B	13	H
14	B	15	F
16	B	17	F
18	D	19	G
20	C	21	G
22	A	23	F
24	B	25	J
26	A	27	J
28	B	29	H
30	A		

31 *Answers will vary.*
The air in the balloon goes down through the hole in the spool and makes a cushion of air between the cardboard square and the table. The hovercraft can move easily on the cushion of air because there is no friction.

page 146
Practice Math Test

1	B	2	H
3	D	4	H
5	C	6	G
7	C	8	H
9	C	10	H
11	A		

12

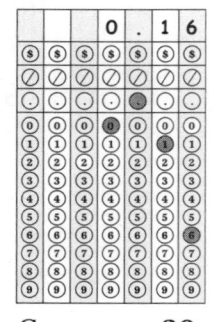

13	G	14	B
15	G	16	B
17	G	18	B
19	G	20	D
21	J	22	B
23	H	24	B
25	H	26	D
27	J		

28

29	C	30	H